ABOUT THE AUTHOR

Angela Carter (1940–1992) was born in Eastbourne and brought up in south Yorkshire. One of Britain's most original and disturbing writers, she read English at Bristol University and wrote her first novel, *Shadow Dance*, in 1965. *The Magic Toyshop* won the John Llewellyn Rhys Prize in 1969 and *Several Perceptions* won the Somerset Maugham Prize in 1968. More novels followed and in 1974 her translation of the fairy tales of Charles Perrault was published, and in the early nineties she edited the *Virago Book of Fairy Tales*. Her journalism appeared in almost every major publication; a collection of the best of these were published by Virago in *Nothing Special* (1982). She also wrote poetry and a film script together with Neil Jordan of her story 'The Company of Wolves'. Her last novel, *Wise Children*, was published to widespread acclaim in 1991. Angela Carter's death at age fifty-one in February 1992 'robbed the English literary scene of one of its most vivacious and compelling voices' – *Independent*.

By Angela Carter

Fiction
Shadow Dance
The Magic Toyshop
Several Perceptions
Heroes and Villains
Love
The Infernal Desire Machines of Doctor Hoffman
The Passion of New Eve
Black Venus's Tale
Nights at the Circus
Wise Children
The Bloody Chamber and Other Stories
Black Venus
American Ghosts & Old World Wonders
Burning Your Boats: the Complete Short Stories
Fireworks
Angela Carter's Book of Wayward Girls and
Wicked Women

Non-Fiction
The Sadeian Woman: An Exercise in Cultural History
Nothing Sacred: Selected Writings
The Virago Book of Fairy Tales (editor)
The Second Virago Book of Fairy Tales (editor)
Angela Carter's Book of Fairy Tales (editor)
Expletives Deleted: Selected Writings

THE SADEIAN WOMAN

WOMAN

AN EXERCISE IN CULTURAL HISTORY

ANGELA CARTER

VIRAGO

First published in Great Britain by Virago Press in 1979
This edition published by Virago Press in 2023

1 3 5 7 9 10 8 6 4 2

A CIP catalogue record for this book
is available from the British Library.

ISBN 978-0-349-01741-9

Typeset in Goudy by M Rules
Printed and bound in Great Britain
by Clays Ltd, Elcograf S.p.A.

Papers used by Virago are from well-managed forests
and other responsible sources.

MIX
Paper from
responsible sources
FSC® C104740

Virago Press
An imprint of
Little, Brown Book Group
Carmelite House
50 Victoria Embankment
London EC4Y 0DZ

An Hachette UK Company
www.hachette.co.uk

www.virago.co.uk

CONTENTS

INTRODUCTORY NOTE

Sade was born in 1740, a great nobleman; and died in 1814, in a lunatic asylum, a poor man. His life spans the entire period of the French Revolution and he died in the same year that Napoleon abdicated and the monarchy was restored to France. He stands on the threshold of the modern period, looking both backward and forwards, at a time when the nature of human nature and of social institutions was debated as freely as it is in our own.

Sade's work concerns the nature of sexual freedom and is of particular significance to women because of his refusal to see female sexuality in relation to its reproductive function, a refusal as unusual in the late eighteenth century as it is now, even if today the function of women as primarily reproductive beings is under question. *The Sadeian Woman* is neither a critical study nor a historical analysis of Sade; it is, rather, a late-twentieth-century interpretation of some of the problems he raises about the culturally determined nature of women and of the relations between men and women that result from it – an opposition which is both cruelly divisive in our common struggle to understand the world, and also, in itself, a profound illumination of the nature of that struggle.

ONE

Polemical Preface:
Pornography in the Service of Women

> Sadism is not a name finally given to a practice as old as Eros; it is a massive cultural fact which appeared precisely at the end of the eighteenth century, and which constitutes one of the greatest conversions of Western imagination: unreason transformed into delirium of the heart, madness of desire, the insane dialogue of love and death in the limitless presumption of appetite.
>
> *Madness and Civilisation*,
> Michel Foucault

> I am not the slave of the Slavery that dehumanised my ancestors.
> *Black Skin White Masks*,
> Frantz Fanon

Pornographers are the enemies of women only because our contemporary ideology of pornography does not encompass the possibility of change, as if we were the slaves of history and not its makers, as if sexual relations were not necessarily an expression of social relations, as if sex itself were an external fact, one as immutable as the weather, creating human practice but never a part of it.

Pornography involves an abstraction of human intercourse in which the self is reduced to its formal elements. In its most basic form, these elements are represented by the probe and the fringed hole, the twin signs of male and female in graffiti, the biological symbols scrawled on the subway poster and the urinal wall, the simplest expression of stark and ineradicable sexual differentiation, a universal pictorial language of lust – or, rather, a language we accept as universal because, since it has always been so, we conclude that it must always remain so.

In the stylisation of graffiti, the prick is always presented erect, in an alert attitude of enquiry or curiosity or affirmation; it points upwards, it asserts. The hole is open, an inert space, like a mouth waiting to be filled. From this elementary iconography may be derived the whole metaphysic of sexual differences – man aspires; woman has no other function but to exist, waiting. The male is positive, an exclamation mark. Woman is negative. Between her legs lies nothing but zero, the sign for nothing, that only becomes something when the male principle fills it with meaning.

Anatomy is destiny, said Freud, which is true enough as far as it goes, but ambiguous. My anatomy is only part of an infinitely complex organisation, my self. The anatomical reductionalism of graffiti, the *reductio ad absurdum* of the bodily differences between men and women, extracts all the evidence of me from myself and leaves behind only a single aspect of my life as a mammal. It enlarges this aspect, simplifies it and then presents it as the most significant aspect of my entire humanity. This is true of all mythologising of sexuality; but graffiti lets it be *seen* to be true. It is the most explicit version of the idea of different sexual essences of men and women, because it is the crudest. In

4

the face of this symbolism, my pretensions to any kind of social existence go for nothing; graffiti directs me back to my mythic generation as a woman and, as a woman, my symbolic value is primarily that of a myth of patience and receptivity, a dumb mouth from which the teeth have been pulled.

Sometimes, especially under the influence of Jung, a more archaic mouth is allowed to exert an atavistic dominance. Then, if I am lucky enough to be taken with such poetic pseudo-seriousness, my nether mouth may be acknowledged as one capable of speech – were there not, of old, divinatory priestesses, female oracles and so forth? Was there not Cassandra, who always spoke the truth, although admittedly in such a way that nobody ever believed her? And that, in mythic terms, is the hell of it. Since that female, oracular mouth is located so near the beastly backside, my vagina might indeed be patronisingly regarded as a speaking mouth, but never one that issues the voice of reason. In this most insulting mythic redefinition of myself, that of occult priestess, I am indeed allowed to speak but only of things that male society does not take seriously. I can hint at dreams, I can even personify the imagination; but that is only because I am not rational enough to cope with reality.

If women allow themselves to be consoled for their culturally determined lack of access to the modes of intellectual debate by the invocation of hypothetical great goddesses, they are simply flattering themselves into submission (a technique often used on them by men). All the mythic versions of women, from the myth of the redeeming purity of the virgin to that of the healing, reconciling mother, are consolatory nonsenses; and consolatory nonsense seems to me a fair definition of myth, anyway. Mother goddesses are just as silly a notion as father gods. If a revival of the myths of these cults gives women emotional satisfaction, it does so at the price of obscuring the real conditions of life. This is why they were invented in the first place.

Myth deals in false universals, to dull the pain of particular circumstances. In no area is this more true than in that of relations between the sexes. Graffiti, the most public form of sexual iconography, one which requires no training or artistic skill in its execution and yet is always assured of an audience, obtains all its effects from these false universals of myth. Its savage denial of the complexity of human relations is also a consolatory nonsense.

In its schema, as in the mythic schema of all relations between men and women, man proposes and woman is disposed of, just as she is disposed of in a rape, which is a kind of physical graffiti, the most extreme reduction of love, in which all humanity departs from the sexed beings. So that, somewhere in the fear of rape, is a more than merely physical terror of hurt and humiliation – a fear of psychic disintegration, of an essential dismemberment, a fear of a loss or disruption of the self which is not confined to the victim alone. Since all pornography derives directly from myth, it follows that its heroes and heroines, from the most gross to the most sophisticated, are mythic abstractions, heroes and heroines of dimension and capacity. Any glimpse of a real man or a real woman is absent from these representations of the archetypal male and female.

The nature of the individual is not resolved into but is ignored by these archetypes, since the function of the archetype is to diminish the unique 'I' in favour of a collective, sexed being which cannot, by reason of its very nature, exist as such because an archetype is only an image that has got too big for its boots and bears, at best, a fantasy relation to reality.

All archetypes are spurious but some are more spurious than others. There is the unarguable fact of sexual differentiation; but, separate from it and only partially derived from it, are the behavioural modes of masculine and feminine, which are culturally defined variables translated in the language of common usage to the status of universals. And these archetypes serve only to confuse the main issue, that relationships between the sexes are determined by history and by the historical fact of the economic dependence of women upon men. This fact is now very largely a fact of the past and, even in the past, was only true for certain social groups and then only at certain periods. Today, most women work before, during and after marriage. Nevertheless, the economic dependence of women remains a believed fiction and is assumed to imply an emotional dependence that is taken for granted as a condition inherent in the natural order of things and so used to console working women for their low wages. They work; see little profit from it; and therefore conclude they cannot really have been working at all.

This confusion as to the experience of reality – that what I know from my experience is true is, in fact, not so – is most apparent, however, in the fantasy love-play of the archetypes, which generations of artists have contrived to make seem so attractive that, lulled by dreams, many women willingly ignore the palpable evidence of their own responses.

In these beautiful encounters, any man may encounter any woman and their personalities are far less important to their copulation than the mere fact of their genders. At the first touch or sigh he, she, is subsumed immediately into a universal. (She, of course, rarely approaches him; that is not part of the fantasy of fulfillment.) She is most immediately and dramatically a woman when she lies beneath a man, and her submission is the apex of his malehood. To show his humility before his own erection, a man must approach a woman on his knees, just as he approaches god. This is the kind of beautiful thought that has bedevilled the history of sex in Judaeo-Christian culture, causing almost as much confusion as the idea that sex is a sin. Some of the scorn heaped on homosexuals may derive from the fact that they do not customarily adopt the mythically correct, sacerdotal position. The same beautiful thought has elevated a Western European convention to the position of the only sanctified sexual position; it fortifies the missionary position with a bizarre degree of mystification. God is invoked as a kind of sexual referee, to assure us, as modern churchmen like to claim in the teeth of two thousand years of Christian sexual repression, that sex is really sacred.

The missionary position has another great asset, from the mythic point of view; it implies a system of relations between the partners that equates the woman to the passive receptivity of the soil, to the richness and fecundity of the earth. A whole range of images poeticises, kitschifies, departicularises intercourse, such as wind beating down corn, rain driving against bending trees, towers falling, all tributes to the freedom and strength of the roving, fecundating, irresistible male principle and the heavy, downward, equally irresistible gravity of the receptive soil. The soil that is, good heavens, myself. It is a most self-enhancing notion; I have almost seduced myself with it. Any woman may manage, in luxurious self-deceit, to feel herself for a little while one with great, creating nature, fertile, open, pulsing, anonymous and so forth. In doing so, she loses herself completely and loses her partner also.

The moment they succumb to this anonymity, they cease to be themselves, with their separate lives and desires; they cease to be the lovers who have met to assuage desire in a reciprocal pact of tenderness, and they engage at once in a spurious charade of maleness and femaleness.

The anonymity of the lovers, whom the act transforms from me and you into they, precludes the expression of ourselves.

So the act is taken away from us even as we perform it.

We become voyeurs upon our own caresses. The act does not acknowledge the participation of the individual, bringing to it a whole life of which the act is only a part. The man and woman, in their particularity, their being, are absent from these representations of themselves as male and female. These tableaux of falsification remove our sexual life from the world, from tactile experience itself. The lovers are lost to themselves in a privacy that does not transcend but deny reality. So the act can never satisfy them, because it does not affect their lives. It occurs in the mythic dream-time of religious ritual.

But our flesh arrives to us out of history, like everything else does. We may believe we fuck stripped of social artifice; in bed, we even feel we touch the bedrock of human nature itself. But we are deceived. Flesh is not an irreducible human universal. Although the erotic relationship may seem to exist freely, on its own terms, among the distorted social relationships of a bourgeois society, it is, in fact, the most self-conscious of all human relationships, a direct confrontation of two beings whose actions in the bed are wholly determined by their acts when they are out of it. If one sexual partner is economically dependent on the other, then the question of sexual coercion, of contractual obligation, raises its ugly head in the very abode of love and inevitably colours the nature of the sexual expression of affection. The marriage bed is a particularly delusive refuge from the world because all wives of necessity fuck by contract. Prostitutes are at least decently paid on the nail and boast fewer illusions about a hireling status that has no veneer of social acceptability, but their services are suffering a decline in demand now that other women have invaded their territory in their own search for a newly acknowledged sexual pleasure. In this period, promiscuous abandon may seem the only type of free exchange.

But no bed, however unexpected, no matter how apparently gratuitous, is free from the de-universalising facts of real life. We do not go to bed in simple pairs; even if we choose not to refer to them, we still drag there with us the cultural impedimenta of our social class, our parents' lives, our bank balances, our sexual and emotional expectations, our whole biographies – all the bits and pieces of our unique existences. These considerations have limited our choice of partners before we have even got them into the bedroom. It was impossible for the Countess in Beaumarchais's *The Marriage of Figaro* to contemplate sleeping with her husband's valet, even though he was clearly the best man available; considerations of social class censored the possibility of sexual attraction between the Countess and Figaro before it could have begun to exist, and if this convention restricted the Countess's activities, it did not affect those of her husband; he happily plotted to seduce his valet's wife. If middle-class Catherine Earnshaw, in Emily

Brontë's *Wuthering Heights*, wants to sleep with Heathcliff, who has the dubious class origins of the foundling, she must not only repress this desire but pay the socially sanctioned price of brain-fever and early death for even contemplating it. Our literature is full, as are our lives, of men and women, but especially women, who deny the reality of sexual attraction and of love because of considerations of class, religion, race and of gender itself.

Class dictates our choice of partners and our choice of positions. When fear, shame and prudery condemn the poor and the ignorant to copulate in the dark, it must be obvious that sexual sophistication is a by-product of education. The primal nakedness of lovers is a phenomenon of the middle-class in cold climates; in northern winters, naked lovers must be able to afford to heat their bedrooms. The taboos regulating the sight of bare flesh are further determined by wider cultural considerations. The Japanese bathed together in the nude for centuries, yet generations of Japanese lovers fucked in kimono, even in the humidity of summer, and did not even remove the combs from their chignons while they did so. And another complication – they did not appreciate the eroticism of the nude; yet they looked at one another's exposed genitalia with a tender readiness that still perturbs the West.

Control of fertility is a by-product of sexual education and of official legislation concerning the availability of cheap or free contraception. Even so, a poor woman may find herself sterilised when all she wanted was an abortion, her fertility taken out of her own control for good by social administrators who have decided that poverty is synonymous with stupidity and a poor woman cannot know her own mind.

The very magical privacy of the bed, the pentacle, may itself only be bought with money, and lack of privacy limits sexual sophistication, which may not be pursued in a room full of children.

Add to these socio-economic considerations the Judaeo-Christian heritage of shame, disgust and morality that stand between the initial urge and the first attainment of this most elementary assertion of the self and it is a wonder anyone in this culture ever learns to fuck at all.

Flesh comes to us out of history; so does the repression and taboo that governs our experience of flesh.

The nature of actual modes of sexual intercourse is determined by historical changes in less intimate human relations, just as the actual nature of men and women is capable of infinite modulations as social structures change. Our knowledge is determined by the social boundaries upon it; for example, Sade, the eighteenth-century lecher, knew that manipulation of the clitoris was the unique key to the female orgasm, but a hundred years later, Sigmund Freud, a Viennese intellectual, did not wish to believe that this grand simplicity was all there was to the business. It was socially permissible for an eighteenth-century aristocrat to sleep with more women than it was for a member of the nineteenth-century bourgeoisie, for one thing, and to retain a genuine curiosity about female sexuality whilst doing so, for another. Yet Freud, the psychoanalyst, can conceive of a far richer notion of human nature as a whole than Sade, the illiberal philosopher, is capable of; the social boundaries of knowledge expand in some areas and contract in others due to historical forces.

Sexuality, in short, is never expressed in a vacuum. Though

the archaic sequence of human life – we are born, we fuck, we reproduce, we die – might seem to be universal experience, its universality is not its greatest significance. Since human beings have invented history, we have also invented those aspects of our lives that seem most immutable, or, rather, have invented the circumstances that determine their nature. Birth and death, the only absolute inescapables, are both absolutely determined by the social context in which they occur. There is no longer an inevitable relationship between fucking and reproducing and, indeed, neither fucking nor reproducing have been activities practised by all men and women at all times, anyway; there has always been the option to abstain, whether it is exercised or not. Women experience sexuality and reproduction quite differently than men do; rich women are more in control of the sequence than poor women and so may actually enjoy fucking and childbirth, when poor women might find them both atrocious simply because they are poor and cannot afford comfort, privacy and paid help.

The notion of a universality of human experience is a confidence trick and the notion of a universality of female experience is a clever confidence trick.

Pornography, like marriage and the fictions of romantic love, assists the process of false universalising. Its excesses belong to that timeless, locationless area outside history, outside geography, where fascist art is born.

Nevertheless, there is no question of an aesthetics of pornography. It can never be art for art's sake. Honourably enough, it is always art with work to do.

Pornographic literature, the specific area of pornography with which we are going to deal, has several functions. On one level, and a level which should not be despised, it might serve as an instruction manual for the inexperienced. But our culture, with its metaphysics of sexuality, relegates the descriptions of the mechanics of sex to crude functionalism; in the sex textbook, intercourse also takes place in a void. So pornography's principal and most humanly significant function is that of arousing sexual excitement. It does this by ignoring the first function; it usually describes the sexual act not in explicit terms – for that might make it seem frightening – but in purely inviting terms.

The function of plot in a pornographic narrative is always the same. It exists purely to provide as many opportunities as possible for the sexual act to take place. There is no room here for tension or the unexpected. We know what is going to happen; that is why we are reading the book. Characterisation is necessarily limited by the formal necessity for the actors to fuck as frequently and as ingeniously as possible. But they do not do so because they are continually consumed by desire; the free expression of desire is as alien to pornography as it is to marriage. In pornography, both men and women fuck because to fuck is their raison d'être. It is their life work.

It follows that prostitutes are favourite heroines of the pornographic writer, though the economic aspects of a prostitute's activity, which is her own main concern in the real world, will be dealt with only lightly. Her labour is her own private business. Work, in this context, is *really* dirty work; it is unmentionable. Even unspeakable. And we may not talk about it because it reintroduces the question of the world. In this privatised universe pleasure is the only work; work itself is unmentionable. To concentrate on the prostitute's trade *as* trade would introduce too much reality into a scheme that is first and foremost one of libidinous fantasy, and pornographic writers, in general, are not concerned with extending the genre in which they work to include a wider view of the world. This is because pornography is the orphan little sister of the arts; its functionalism renders it suspect, more applied art than fine art, and so its very creators rarely take it seriously.

Fine art, that exists for itself alone, is art in a final state of impotence. If nobody, including the artist, acknowledges art as a means of *knowing* the world, then art is relegated to a kind of rumpus room of the mind and the irresponsibility of the artist and the irrelevance of art to actual living becomes part and parcel of the practice of art. Nevertheless, pornographic writing retains this in common with all literature – that it turns the flesh into word. This is the real transformation the text performs upon libidinous fantasy.

The verbal structure is in itself reassuring. We know we are not dealing with real flesh or anything like it, but with a cunningly articulated verbal simulacrum which has the power to arouse, but not, in itself, to assuage desire. At this point, the reader, the consumer, enters the picture; reflecting the social dominance which affords him the opportunity to purchase the flesh of other people as if it were meat, the reader or consumer of pornography is usually a man who subscribes to a particular social fiction of manliness. His belief in this fiction prevents him from realising that, when he picks up a dirty book, he engages in a game with his own desire and with his own solitude, both of which he endlessly titillates but never openly confronts.

Therefore a cerebral insatiability, unacknowledged yet implicit, is a characteristic of pornography, which always throws the reader back on his own resources, since it convinces him of the impotence of his desire that the book cannot in itself assuage, at the same time as he solaces that loneliness through the medium of the fantasy extracted from the fiction.

The one-to-one relation of the reader with the book is never more apparent than in the reading of a pornographic novel, since it is virtually impossible to forget oneself in relation to the text. In pornographic literature, the text has a gap left in it on purpose so that the reader may, in imagination, step inside it. But the activity the text describes, into which the reader enters, is not a whole world into which the reader is absorbed and, as they say, 'taken out of himself'. It is one basic activity extracted from the world in its totality in such a way that the text constantly reminds the reader of his own troubling self, his own reality – and the limitations of that reality since, however much he wants to fuck the willing women or men in his story, he cannot do so but must be content with some form of substitute activity. (The fictional maleness of the pornography consumer encompasses the butch hero of homosexual pornography; it is a *notion* of masculinity unrelated to practice.)

The privacy of the reader is invaded by his own desires, which reach out towards the world beyond the book he is reading. Yet they are short-circuited by the fantastic nature of the gratification promised by the text, which denies to flesh all its intransigence, indeed its sexed quality, since sexuality is a quality made manifest in being, and pornography can only allow its phantoms to exist in the moment of sexual excitation; they cannot engage in the wide range of activity in the real world in which sexual performance is not the supreme business of all people at all times.

Yet the gripping nature of pornography, its directly frontal assault upon the senses of the reader, its straightforward engagement of him at a non-intellectual level, its *sensationalism*, suggest the methodology of propaganda. Indeed, pornography is basically propaganda for fucking, an activity, one would have thought, that did not need much advertising in itself, because most people want to do it as soon as they know how.

The denial of the social fact of sexuality in pornography is made explicit in its audience. Produced in the main by men for an all-male clientele, suggesting certain analogies with a male brothel, access to pornography is usually denied to women at any level, often on the specious grounds that women do not find descriptions of the sexual act erotically stimulating. Yet if pornography is produced by men for a male audience, it is exclusively concerned with relations between the sexes and even the specialised area of homosexual pornography divides its actors into sexual types who might roughly be defined as 'masculine' and 'feminine'. So all pornography suffers the methodological defects of a manual of navigation written by and for landlubbers.

Many pornographic novels are written in the first person as if by a woman, or use a woman as the focus of the narrative; but this device only reinforces the male orientation of the fiction. John Cleland's *Fanny Hill* and the anonymous *The Story of O*, both classics of the genre, appear in this way to describe a woman's mind through the fiction of her sexuality. This technique ensures that the gap left in the text is of just the right size for the reader to insert his prick into, the exact dimensions, in fact, of Fanny's vagina or of O's anus. Pornography engages the reader in a most intimate fashion before it leaves him to his own resources. This gap in the text may also be just the size of the anus or mouth of a young man, subsuming him, too, to this class that is most present in its absence, the invisible recipients of the pornographic tribute, the mental masturbatory objects.

So pornography reinforces the false universals of sexual archetypes because it denies, or doesn't have time for, or can't find room for, or, because of its underlying ideology, ignores, the social context in which sexual activity takes place, that modifies the very nature of that activity. Therefore pornography must always have the false simplicity of fable; the abstraction of the flesh involves the mystification of the flesh. As it reduces the actors in the sexual drama to instruments of pure function, so the pursuit of pleasure becomes in itself a metaphysical quest. The pornographer, in spite of himself, becomes a metaphysician when he states that the friction of penis in orifice is the supreme matter of the world, for which the world is well lost; as he says so, the world vanishes.

Pornography, like satire, has an inbuilt reactionary mechanism. Its effect depends on the notion that the nature of man is invariable and cannot be modified by changes in his social institutions. The primordial itch in the groin existed before multinational business corporations and the nuclear family and will outlast them just as it illicitly dominates them. The disruptiveness of sexuality, its inability to be contained, the overflowing of the cauldron of id – these are basic invariables of sexuality, opines the pornographer, and in itself pornography is a satire on human pretensions. The judge conceals his erection beneath his robes of office as he passes judgement on the whore. The cabinet minister slips away from his office early to visit the call girl. The public executioner ejaculates as the neck of his victim snaps. And we laugh wryly at the omnipotence of Old Adam, how he will always, somehow or other, get his way; and we do ourselves and Old Adam the grossest injustice when we grant him so much power, when we reduce sexuality to the status of lowest common denominator without asking ourselves what preconceptions make us think it should be so.

Since sexuality is as much a social fact as it is a human one, it will therefore change its nature according to changes in social conditions. If we could restore the context of the world to the embraces of these shadows then, perhaps, we could utilise their activities to obtain a fresh perception of the world and, in some sense, transform it. The sexual act in pornography exists as a metaphor for what people do to one another, often in the cruellest sense; but the present business of the pornographer is to suppress the metaphor as much as he can and leave us with a handful of empty words.

Pornographic pictures, movies and narrative fiction are the pure forms of sexual fiction, of the fiction *of* sex, where this operation of alienation takes place most visibly. But all art which contains elements of eroticism (eroticism, the pornography of the elite) contains the possibility of the same methodology – that is, writing that can 'pull' a reader just as a woman 'pulls' a man or a man 'pulls' a woman.

And all such literature has the potential to force the reader to reassess his relation to his own sexuality, which is to say to his own primary being, through the mediation of the image or the text. This is true for women also, perhaps especially so, as soon as we realise the way pornography reinforces the archetypes of her negativity and that it does so simply because most pornography remains in the service of the status quo. And that is because its elementary metaphysic gets in the way of real life and prevents us seeing real life. If the world has been lost, the world may not be reassessed. Libidinous fantasy in a vacuum is the purest, but most affectless, form of day-dreaming. So pornography in general serves to defuse the explosive potential of all sexuality and that is the main reason why it is made by and addressed to the politically dominant minority in the world, as an instrument of repression, not only of women, but of men too. Pornography keeps sex in its place. That is, under the carpet. That is, outside everyday human intercourse.

The sexuality of the blue movie queen, contained by her social subservience, exhibits no menace. Linda Lovelace does not believe in the Women's Liberation Movement; how could she? Fanny Hill gladly gives up the dominant role of mistress for the subservient role of wife and hands to her Charles all her hard-earned money too, which is an infinitely more far-reaching gesture of submission than that of accepting his sexual mastery and opting for domestic monogamy and motherhood under his exclusive economic sanction. Fanny knows in her heart that her Charles is really her last, most efficient, pimp. O, less complex because her economic means of support are not explored as closely as Cleland explores Fanny's, is more content simply to rejoice in her chains, a model for all women.

It is fair to say that, when pornography serves – as with very rare exceptions it always does – to reinforce the prevailing system of values and ideas in a given society, it is tolerated; and when it does not, it is banned. (This already suggests there are more reasons than those of public decency for the banning of the work of Sade for almost two hundred years; only at the time of the French Revolution and at the present day have his books been available to the general public.) Therefore an increase of pornography on the market, within the purchasing capacity of the common man, and especially the beginning of a type of pornography modelled on that provided for the male consumer but directed at women, does not mean an increase in sexual licence, with the reappraisal of social mores such licence, if it is real, necessitates. It might only indicate a more liberal attitude to masturbation, rather than to fucking, and reinforce a sollipsistic concentration on the relationship with the self, which is a fantasy one at the best of times.

When pornography abandons its quality of existential solitude and moves out of the kitsch area of timeless, placeless fantasy and into the real world, then it loses its function of safety valve. It begins to comment on real relations in the real world. Therefore, the more pornographic writing aquires the techniques of real literature, of real art, the more deeply subversive it is likely to be in that the more likely it is to affect the reader's perceptions of the world. The text that had heretofore opened up creamily to him, in a dream, will gather itself together and harshly expel him into the anguish of actuality.

There is a liberal theory that art disinfects eroticism of its latent subversiveness, and pornography that is also art loses its shock and its magnetism, becomes 'safe'. The truth of this is that once pornography is labelled 'art' or 'literature' it is stamped with the approval of an elitist culture and many ordinary people will avoid it on principle, out of a fear of being bored. But the more the literary arts of plotting and characterisation are used to shape the material of pornography, the more the pornographer himself is faced with the moral contradictions inherent in real sexual encounters. He will find himself in a dilemma; to opt for the world or to opt for the wet dream?

Out of this dilemma, the moral pornographer might be born.

The moral pornographer would be an artist who uses pornographic material as part of the acceptance of the logic of a world of absolute sexual licence for all the genders, and projects a model of the way such a world might work. A moral pornographer might use pornography as a critique of current relations between the sexes. His business would be the total demystification of the flesh and the subsequent revelation, through the infinite modulations of the sexual act, of the real relations of man and his kind. Such a pornographer would not be the enemy of women, perhaps because he might begin to penetrate to the heart of the contempt for women that distorts our culture even as he entered the realms of true obscenity as he describes it.

But the pornographer's more usual business is to assert that the function of flesh is pure pleasure, which is itself a mystification of a function a great deal more complex, apart from raising the question of the nature of pleasure itself. However, the nature of pleasure is not one with which the pornographer often concerns himself; for him, sexual pleasure is a given fact, a necessary concomitant of the juxtaposition of bodies.

It is at this point that he converts the sexed woman, living, breathing, troubling, into a desexed hole and the breathing, living, troubling man into nothing but a probe; pornography becomes a form of pastoral, sex an engaging and decorative activity that may be performed without pain, soil, sweat or effect, and its iconography a very suitable subject for informal murals in public places. If, that is, the simplest descriptions of sex did not also rouse such complex reactions.

And that is because sexual relations between men and women always render explicit the nature of social relations in the society in which they take place and, if described explicitly, will form a critique of those relations, even if that is not and never has been the intention of the pornographer.

So, whatever the surface falsity of pornography, it is impossible for it to fail to reveal sexual reality at an unconscious level, and this reality may be very unpleasant indeed, a world away from official reality.

A male-dominated society produces a pornography of universal female aquiescence. Or, most delicious titillation, of compensatory but spurious female dominance. Miss Stern with her rods and whips, Our Lady of Pain in her leather visor and her boots with sharp, castratory heels, is a true fantasy, a distorted version of the old saying 'The hand that rocks the cradle rules the world.' This whip hand rocks the cradle in which her customer dreams but it does nothing else. Miss Stern's dominance exists only in the bedroom. She may utilise apparatus that invokes heaven, hell and purgatory for her client, she may utterly ravage his body, martyrise him, shit on him, piss on him, but her cruelty is only the manifestation of the victim or patient's guilt before the fact of his own sexuality, of which he is ashamed. She is not cruel for her own sake, or for her own gratification. She is most truly subservient when most apparently dominant; Miss Stern and her pretended victim have established a mutually degrading pact between them and she in her weird garb is mutilated more savagely by the erotic violence she perpetrates than he by the pain he undergoes, since his pain is in the nature of a holiday from his life, and her cruelty an economic fact of her real life, so much hard work. You can describe their complicity in a pornographic novel but to relate it to her mortgage, her maid's salary and her laundry bills is to use the propaganda technique of pornography to express a view of the world, which deviates from the notion that all this takes place in a kindergarten of soiled innocence. A kindergarten? Only small children, in our society, do not need to work.

The pornographer who consciously utilises the propaganda, the 'grabbing' effect of pornography to express a view of the world that transcends this kind of innocence will very soon find himself in deep political water for he will begin to find himself describing the real conditions of the world in terms of sexual encounters, or even find that the real nature of these encounters illuminates the world itself; the world turns into a gigantic brothel, the area of our lives where we believed we possessed most freedom is seen as the most ritually circumscribed.

Nothing exercises such power over the imagination as the nature of sexual relationships, and the pornographer has it in his power to become a terrorist of the imagination, a sexual guerrilla whose purpose is to overturn our most basic notions of these relations, to reinstitute sexuality as a primary mode of being rather than a specialised area of vacation from being and to show that the everyday meetings in the marriage bed are parodies of their own pretensions, that the freest unions may contain the seeds of the worst exploitation. Sade became a terrorist of the imagination in this way, turning the unacknowledged truths of the encounters of sexuality into a cruel festival at which women are the prime sacrificial victims when they are not the ritual murderesses themselves, the ewe lamb and Miss Stern together, alike only in that they always remain under the constant surveillance of the other half of mankind.

The pornographer as terrorist may not think of himself as a friend of women; that may be the last thing on his mind. But he will always be our unconscious ally because he begins to approach some kind of emblematic truth, whereas the lackey pornographer, like the devious fellows who write love stories for women's magazines, that softest of all forms of pornography, can only do harm. But soon, however permissive censorship may be, he will invade the area in which censorship operates most defensibly, that of erotic violence.

This area of taboo remains theoretically inviolate even though violence, for its own sake, between men, escapes censorship altogether. The machine-gun of the gangster can rake as many innocent victims as the writer or film-maker pleases, the policeman can blast as many wrongdoers to extinction as serves to demonstrate the superiority of his institutions. Novels and movies about warfare use violent death, woundings and mutilations as a form of decoration, butch embroidery upon a male surface. Violence, the convulsive form of the active, male principle, is a matter for men, whose sex gives them the right to inflict pain as a sign of mastery and the masters have the right to wound one another because that only makes us fear them more, that they can give and receive pain like the lords of creation. But to show, in art, erotic violence committed by men upon women cuts too near the bone, and will be condemned out of hand.

Perhaps it reveals too clearly that violence has always been the method by which institutions demonstrate their superiority. It can become too vicious a reminder of the mutilations our society inflicts upon women and the guilt that exacerbates this savagery. It suggests, furthermore, that male political dominance might be less a matter of moral superiority than of crude brute force and this would remove a degree of glamour from the dominance itself.

There is more to it than that, though. The whippings, the beatings, the gougings, the stabbings of erotic violence reawaken the memory of the social fiction of the female wound, the bleeding scar left by her castration, which is a psychic fiction as deeply at the heart of Western culture as the myth of Oedipus, to which it is related in the complex dialectic of imagination and reality that produces culture. Female castration is an imaginary fact that pervades the whole of men's attitude towards women and our attitude to ourselves, that transforms women from human beings into wounded creatures who were born to bleed.

It is a great shame we can forbid these bleedings in art but not in life, for the beatings, the rapes and the woundings take place in a privacy beyond the reach of official censorship. It is also in private that the unacknowledged psychological mutilations performed in the name of love take place.

Sade is the connoisseur of these mutilations. He is an extreme writer and he describes a society and a system of social relations *in extremis*, those of the last years of the ancien régime in France. The stories of Justine and Juliette are set at a time immediately preceding the French Revolution. *The Hundred and Twenty Days at Sodom* is set in the seventeenth century. Its heroes have financed their murderous holiday by vast profits made from the Thirty Years War. *Philosophy in the Boudoir* takes place some time between 1789 and 1793; outside the room in which the action of this dramatic interlude takes place, they are selling revolutionary pamphlets on the steps of the Palace of

Equality but the actors in the boudoir are aristocrats, members of a privileged class. In all this fiction, Sade is working primarily in the mode of pornogrsphy; he utilised this mode to make a particularly wounding satire on mankind, and the historical time in which the novels are set is essential to the satire.

But Sade is unusual amongst both satirists and pornographers, not only because he goes further than most satirists and pornographers, but because he is capable of believing, even if only intermittently, that it is possible to radically transform society and, with it, human nature, so that the Old Adam, exemplified in God, the King and the Law, the trifold masculine symbolism of authority, will take his final departure from amongst us. Only then will freedom be possible; until then, the freedom of one class, or sex, or individual necessitates the unfreedom of others.

But his work as a pornographer is more descriptive and diagnostic than proscriptive and prophetic. He creates, not an artificial paradise of gratified sexuality but a model of hell, in which the gratification of sexuality involves the infliction and the tolerance of extreme pain. He describes sexual relations in the context of an unfree society as the expression of pure tyranny, usually by men upon women, sometimes by men upon men, sometimes by women upon men and other women; the one constant to all Sade's monstrous orgies is that the whip hand is always the hand with the real political power and the victim is a person who has little or no power at all, or has had it stripped from him. In this schema, male means tyrannous and female means martyrised, no matter what the official genders of the male and female beings are.

He is uncommon amongst pornographers in that he rarely, if

ever, makes sexual activity seem immediately attractive as such. Sade has a curious ability to render every aspect of sexuality suspect, so that we see how the chaste kiss of the sentimental lover differs only in degree from the vampirish love-bite that draws blood, we understand that a disinterested caress is only quantitatively different from a disinterested flogging. For Sade, all tenderness is false, a deceit, a trap; all pleasure contains within itself the seeds of atrocities; all beds are minefields. So the virtuous Justine is condemned to spend a life in which there is not one single moment of enjoyment; only in this way can she retain her virtue. Whereas the wicked Juliette, her sister and antithesis, dehumanises herself completely in the pursuit of pleasure.

The simple perversions, available in any brothel, documented in the first book of *The Hundred and Twenty Days at Sodom*, will insatiably elaborate, will never suffice in themselves, will culminate in the complex and deathly rites of the last book, which concludes in a perfectly material hell. The final passion recounted by the sexual lexicographer, Madame Desgranges, is called the Hell-game; its inventor, assisted by torturers disguised as demons, himself pretends to be the devil.

In the perpetual solitude of their continually refined perversions, in an absolute egotism, Sade's libertines regulate and maintain a society external to them, where the institutions of which they are the embodiment are also perversions.

These libertines are great aristocrats, landowners, bankers, judges, archbishops, popes and certain women who have become very rich through prostitution, speculation, murder and usury. They have the tragic style and the infernal loquacity of the damned; and they have no inner life, no introspection.

Their actions sum them up completely. They are in exile from the world in their abominable privilege, at the same time as they control the world.

Sade's heroines, those who become libertines, accept damnation, by which I mean this exile from human life, as a necessary fact of life. This is the nature of the libertine. They model themselves upon libertine men, though libertinage is a condition that all the sexes may aspire to. So Sade creates a museum of woman-monsters. He cuts up the bodies of women and reassembles them in the shapes of his own delirium. He renews all the ancient wounds, every one, and makes them bleed again as if they will never stop bleeding.

From time to time, he leaves off satire long enough to posit a world in which nobody need bleed. But only a violent transformation of this world and a fresh start in an absolutely egalitarian society would make this possible. Nevertheless, such a transformation might be possible; at this point, Sade becomes a Utopian. His Utopianism, however, takes the form of Kafka's: 'There *is* hope – but not for us.' The title of the pamphlet describing the Sadeian Utopia inserted in *Philosophy in the Boudoir* is: *Yet Another Effort, Frenchmen, If You Would Become Republicans*. It is possible, but improbable, that effort will be made; perhaps those who make it will have hope.

Sade describes the condition of women in the genre of the pornography of sexual violence but believed it would only be through the medium of sexual violence that women might heal themselves of their socially inflicted scars, in a praxis of destruction and sacrilege. He cites the flesh as existential verification in itself, in a rewriting of the Cartesian cogito: '*I fuck therefore I am*'. From this axiom, he constructs a diabolical lyricism of fuckery, since the acting-out of a total sexuality in a repressive society turns all eroticism into violence, makes of sexuality itself a permanent negation. Fucking, says Sade, is the basis of all human relationships but the activity parodies all human relations because of the nature of the society that creates and maintains those relationships.

He enlarges the relation between activity and passivity in the sexual act to include tyranny and the acceptance of physical and political oppression. The great men in his novels, the statesmen, the princes, the popes, are the cruellest by far and their sexual voracity is a kind of pure destructiveness; they would like to fuck the world and fucking, for them, is the enforcement of annihilation. Their embraces strangle, their orgasms appear to detonate their partners. But his great women, Juliette, Clairwil, the Princess Borghese, Catherine the Great of Russia, Charlotte of Naples, are even more cruel still since, once they have tasted power, once they know how to use their sexuality as an instrument of aggression, they use it to extract vengeance for the humiliations they were forced to endure as the passive objects of the sexual energy of others.

A free woman in an unfree society will be a monster. Her freedom will be a condition of personal privilege that deprives those on which she exercises it of their own freedom. The most extreme kind of this deprivation is murder. These women murder.

The sexual behaviour of these women, like that of their men, is a mirror of their inhumanity, a magnified relation of the ambivalence of the word 'to fuck', in its twinned meanings of sexual intercourse and despoliation: 'a fuck-up', 'to fuck something up', 'he's fucked'.

Women do not normally fuck in the active sense. They are fucked in the passive tense and hence automatically fucked-up, done over, undone. Whatever else he says or does not say, Sade declares himself unequivocally for the right of women to fuck – as if the period in which women fuck aggressively, tyrannously and cruelly will be a necessary stage in the development of a general human consciousness of the nature of fucking; that if it is not egalitarian, it is unjust. Sade does not suggest this process as such; but he urges women to fuck as actively as they are able, so that powered by their enormous and hitherto untapped sexual energy they will then be able to fuck their way into history and, in doing so, change it.

One of Sade's singularities is that he offers an absolutely sexualised view of the world, a sexualisation that permeates everything, much as his atheism does and, since he is not a religious man but a political man, he treats the facts of female sexuality not as a moral dilemma but as a political reality.

In fact, he treats all sexuality as a political reality and that is inevitable, because his own sexuality brought him directly against the law. He spent the greater part of his adult life in confinement because his own sexual tastes overrode his socialisation; his perversion has entered the dictionary under his own name.

Although he documented his sexual fantasies with an unequalled diligence, and these fantasies delight in the grisliest tortures (even if, in the context of his fictions, he creates an inverted ethical superstructure to legitimise these cruelties), his own sexual practice in life remains relatively obscure. From the evidence of the two court cases in which he was involved, the affair of Rose Keller in 1768 and the charges made against him by a group of Marseilles prostitutes in 1772, he seems to have enjoyed both giving and receiving whippings; voyeurism; anal intercourse, both active and passive; and the presence of an audience at these activities. These are not particularly unusual sexual preferences, though they are more common as fantasies, and are always very expensive if purchased. When they take place in private, the law usually ignores them even when they are against the law, just as it turns a blind eye to wife beating and recreational bondage. Sade, however, seems to have been incapable of keeping his vices private, as if he was aware of their exemplary nature and, perhaps, since the notion of sin, of transgression, was essential to his idea of pleasure, which is always intellectual, never sensual, he may have needed to invoke the punishment of which he consciously denied the validity before he could feel the act itself had been accomplished.

The Rose Keller affair in particular has a curious quality of theatre, of the acting-out of a parable of sex and money. This woman, the thirty-six-year-old widow of a pastry cook, was begging in Paris on Easter Sunday, a day of special significance to the anti-clerical Sade; a day that cried out to be desecrated. According to the deposition she later gave the police, a gentleman, well-dressed, even handsome, approached her in a public square and suggested she might like to earn herself a crown. When she concurred, he took her to a room in a private house; whipped her; gave her food and offered her money, both of which she refused. Then he locked her in the room but she soon escaped through the window and went to tell her tale. Sade admitted freely that he had indeed hired her and whipped her but he said that Rose Keller had known perfectly well he did not intend her to sweep his house, as she claimed, and they had agreed beforehand she would go off with him for a session of debauchery. The matter was settled out of court. Rose Keller was persuaded to withdraw her charge on a payment of an enormous indemnity of two thousand four hundred francs and expenses of seven louis d'or for dressings and ointments for her wounds.

The affair enchants me. It has the completeness and the lucidity of a script by Brecht. A woman of the third estate, a beggar, the poorest of the poor, turns the very vices of the rich into weapons to wound them with. In the fictions he is going to write, Sade will make La Dubois, the brigand chief, say that the callousness of the rich justifies the crimes of the poor; Rose Keller, who expected, perhaps, to have sex with the Marquis but for whom the whip came as a gratuitous, unexpected and unwelcome surprise, turns her hand to blackmail and who can blame her? An ironic triumph for the beggar woman; the victim turned victor.

Sade himself, at this point, is by no means the plain Citizen Sade he became after the French Revolution. He is Donatien-Alphonse-François, Marquis de Sade, Seigneur of Saumane and of La Coste, with other lands in Bresse, Bugey, Valromey and Gex – he owns most of Provence, with sizeable chunks of other parts of France and, if the rents from his tenants are not always forthcoming, he remains good for credit in spite of his extravagances for, besides, he has a rich wife. His title of nobility dates from the twelfth century; he is related to the royal family; there is nothing in his life that does not convince him the world owes him a living and that he can do as he pleases, except the protests of a beggar woman who objected to being whipped even though he gave her bread and beef and offered her money.

Sade is not yet Sade; he is the Marquis. He is the very type of aristocrat who provoked the vengeance of the revolutionaries.

Four years later, he took a box of aniseed balls flavoured with cantharides with him to a brothel in Marseilles and fed the girls with them, to make them fart, which he enjoyed. There was a good deal of whipping and his valet, who accompanied him, buggered him but the girls, cannily, refused to be buggered because they knew they could get into trouble for it. Later that day, the girls who had eaten the sweets began to vomit. One girl, Marguerite Coste, thought she had been poisoned and went to the magistrate.

The public prosecutor issued warrants for the arrest of the Marquis and his valet, Latour, but they had fled from the Sade ancestral mansion, La Coste, some miles from Avignon. They were tried in absentia and found guilty of 'poisoning and sodomy', although the girls were all quite well by now. In absentia, both men were burned in effigy at Aix-en-Provence. Sodomy was at that time a capital crime in France.

If a brothel is a fine place in which to learn misogyny, it is inevitable that Sade, the frequenter of brothels, treated his wife, the unfortunate Renée Pélagie de Montreuil, abominably, teasing her, ignoring her, impregnating her, forcing her to pimp for him and to take part in his orgies, persuading her to pay off the outraged fathers whose daughters he had seduced, scandalously running off with her own sister and, when his adventures ended in prison, further tormenting her with ingenious jealousies. But their married life began badly; without their own consent. Renée Pélagie was a rich bourgeois and Sade an aristocrat with a perennial problem of funding his extravagances. Their two families arranged the match as a business contract, Renée

Pélagie's expectations in exchange for Sade's title, although it seems both knew quite well that Sade had already engaged himself to another woman at the time of the betrothal. Nevertheless, they were married and Renée Pélagie did not leave him until 1790, after twenty-seven years of a marriage the rigours of which must have been eased by Sade's lengthy imprisonment.

The same year that Renée Pélagie finally abandoned him, Sade met a young actress, Constance Quesnet, whose husband, a draper, had recently deserted her and her young son. To complicate the question of his misogyny, Sade remained devoted to this young woman from their meeting until his death some twenty years later, although they were very poor and often separated by force of circumstance and the need to earn a living. He nicknamed this young woman 'Sensitivity' and dedicated *Justine* to her, perhaps an ambivalent gesture. Yet it is not so much sexual abnormality and ambivalence towards women that are the keys to Sade's bleak imaginary universe; it is the combination of sexual obsession – for he was undoubtedly obsessed with sex to a most unusual degree – and imprisonment.

He first went to prison in 1772, at the age of thirty-two, for five months. He had fled the Marseilles affair to Chambéry, in Savoy, then under the control of the King of Sardinia. As if to extract the final ounce of scandal and retribution from the notorious business, he had chosen to elope with his sister-in-law, Anne de Launay – thus, according to the Catholic church, committing incest. Her outraged mother, his mother-in-law, personally requested the King of Sardinia for his arrest and he was sent to the Fortress of Miolans, to escape shortly afterwards. This period of freedom lasted for five years. In June 1778, he returned to Aix-en-Provence for a retrial of the Marseilles poisoning charges. Since the poisoned women had long ago recovered and were now all alive and well, the charge of poisoning was dropped; the accusation of sodomy was withdrawn by the girls. The charge was altered to one of 'debauchery and excessive licentiousness', for which Sade received a public admonition; was fined; and ordered to keep away from Marseilles for three years. In fact, he spent all those years and many more in prison, under a *lettre de cachet* obtained by Madame de Montreil which meant he could be kept in preventive detention, without trial, for an indefinite time. In Sade's case, this was thirteen years.

Except for a charge of moderatism brought against him under the Terror because of his opposition to the death penalty, he was never again publicly charged with any further offence. Rather than his misdeeds, it seems it was the ferocity of his imagination that led to his confinement. His was a peculiarly modern fate, to be imprisoned without trial for crimes that existed primarily in the mind. It is not surprising that *Justine*, with its dominant images of the trial and the castle, recalls Kafka, nor that it arrives to us out of the confinement of its creator at the beginning of the modern period of which it is one of the seminal, if forbidden, books. Sadism, suggests Michel Foucault, is not a sexual perversion but a cultural fact; the consciousness of the 'limitless presumption of the appetite'. Sade's work, with its compulsive attraction for the delinquent imagination of the romantics, has been instrumental in shaping aspects of the modern sensibility; its paranoia, its despair, its sexual terrors, its omnivorous egocentricity, its tolerance of massacre, holocaust, annihilation.

It was prison, the experience of oppression, that transformed the rake into the philosopher, the man of the Age of Reason into the prophet of the age of dissolution, of our own time, the time of the assassins. Deprived of the fact of flesh, he concentrated his notable sexual energy on a curious task of sublimation, a project that involved simultaneously creating and destroying that which he could no longer possess, the flesh, the world, love, in a desolate charnel house of the imagination. It is as well to remember that, when given the opportunity of carrying out this project in practice during the Reign of Terror, he rejected it, at the price of further confinement.

Although Sade's sexual practices would hardly be punished so severely today (and it was punishment that inflamed his sexual imagination to the grossest extent) his sexual imagination would always be of a nature to violate any law that governed any society that retained the notions of crime and punishment. This would be especially true of those societies that most rigorously practice punitive justice, that habitually utilise legislative murder, that is, capital punishment, flogging, mutilation and torture as methods of punishment and intimidation towards their members. For these legal crimes to be described by an honest pervert, or a moral pornographer, as 'pleasure' is to let the cat out of the bag; if Sade is to be castigated for tastes he exercised only in the privacy of his mind or with a few well-paid auxiliaries, then the hanging judge, the birching magistrate, the military torturer with his hoods and his electrodes, the flogging schoolmaster, the brutal husband must also be acknowledged as perverts to whom, in our own criminal folly, we have given a licence to practice upon the general public. Since Sade had no such licence, and, indeed, deplored the fact that licences were granted, his imagination took sexual violence to an extreme that may, in a human being, only be accompanied by an extreme of misanthropy, self-disgust and despair.

His solitude is the perpetual companion and daily horror of the prisoner, whose final place of confinement is the self. 'When I have inspired universal disgust and horror, then I will have conquered solitude', said Baudelaire, who read Sade again and again. Sade projects this diabolic solitude as an absolute egoism; that is the result of thirteen years' solitary meditation on the world. The desires of his imaginary libertines may no longer be satisfied by flesh; flesh becomes an elaborate metaphor for sexual abuse. World, flesh and the devil fuse; when an atheist casts a cool eye on the world, he must always find Satan a more likely hypothesis as ruling principle than a Saviour. Criminality may present itself as a kind of saintly self-mastery, an absolute rejection of hypocrisy. Sade directly influenced Baudelaire; he is also the spiritual ancestor of Genet. Swift saw mankind rolling in a welter of shit, as Sade does, but Sade's satire upon man is far blacker and more infernal than Swift's – for Sade, mankind doesn't roll in shit because mankind is disgusting, but because mankind has overweening aspirations to the superhuman. Of his own contemporaries, he has most in common with the painter Goya; of our contemporaries, the polymorphous perversity and the intense isolation of his characters recall William Burroughs. If Sade is the last, bleak, disillusioned voice of the Enlightenment, he is the avatar of the nihilism of the late twentieth century. His overt misogyny is a single strand in a total revulsion against a mankind of whom, unlike Swift, he cannot delude himself he is not a member.

During the thirteen years in prison, he compiled that immense taxonomy of all the inhumane functions of the sexuality of what the sexual radical, Norman O. Brown, calls 'the immortal child within us', to which Sade gave the title *The Hundred and Twenty Days at Sodom*. He rolled up the manuscript and hid it in a hole in the wall of his cell in the Bastille, where he was now lodged, shortly before July 2 1789. On this day, he was observed shouting through his window that the prisoners in the Bastille were having their throats cut and he should be released; he judged, accurately, that one at least of the cities of the plain was shortly about to suffer a mortal shock. Sade was immediately transferred from the Bastille to the Asylum of Charenton, a hospital for madmen and epileptics, a place to which he would return, to prevent him from further inciting the crowd to storm the prison. They stormed it of their own accord on July 14, the day on which modern history begins.

He was released from Charenton nine months later, as poor as he had once been rich, and signed away his titles to become Citizen Sade. He took up a modest bureaucratic role in the revolutionary government of Paris. Briefly, during the Terror, he acted as a judge and went to prison again for lenience but they soon let him out. It was Napoleon who sent him to prison for the last time, after they found the manuscript copy of *Justine* in Sade's own hand at his publishers. Sade had said he would gladly be a martyr for atheism, if any were needed; to be a martyr for pornography may have struck him as a less glorious fate. Anyway, he always strenuously denied he had written *Justine* and, indeed, all the works by which he has acquired such lasting if scabrous fame.

Sade was transferred speedily from his last prison to the Asylum of Charenton, again, in 1803. His condition was diagnosed as 'sexual dementia', a diagnosis as therapeutically dubious then as now. Nobody considered him mad in everyday terms; nevertheless, he must be put away for the protection of society and there he stayed, in relative comfort, surrounded by books, accompanied by Madame Quesnet, his mistress, posing as his daughter, until he died in 1814. The biographical facts of Sade's life are fully recounted in Gilbert Lely's monumental biography; I don't propose to deal with them any more fully. It was a curious life and its intellectual terms of reference may be found among the books included in the inventory of his effects at Charenton; they include the complete works of Jean-Jacques Rousseau, *The Princess of Cleves*, *Don Quixote* and the 1785 edition of Voltaire in eighty-nine volumes. It is of this world of reason that Sade produces a critique in the guise of a pornographic vision; his heroine, the terrible Juliette, can say, as a hero of Voltaire might: 'I have no light to guide me but my reason.' Yet rationality without humanism founders on itself. On the title page of *Les Liaisons Dangereuses*, Laclos put a quotation from Rousseau's *La Nouvelle Heloise*: 'I have seen the manners of my time and I have published these letters.' Sade might have said that, of the novel *La Nouvelle Justine*, whose title teasingly echoes that of Rousseau's. His fiction blends the picaresque narrative of the late sixteenth and early seventeenth century with the fictions of moral critique of his own youth, and adds to them the sharp outlines of the nightmare.

Sade. An unusual man: aristocrat; atheist; sodomite; novelist; old lag; dramatist; flagellant; glutton; master, as André Breton was the first to point out in his *Anthologie de L'Humeur*

Noir, of black humour. This man who was capable of inventing the most atrocious massacres felt sick when he smelt the blood from the guillotine. This curious and self-contradictory person placed pornography at the service of the French Revolution in the shape of the lengthy, picaresque double novel: *The Adventures of Justine and of Juliette, Her Sister*, and the three different versions of *Justine*. The manuscript of *The Hundred and Twenty Days at Sodom* was lost, to Sade's great regret, and not discovered again until the twentieth century. *Philosophy in the Boudoir* was written in 1795. The rest of his pornographic writing has been lost or destroyed. His voluminous other writings, plays, moral tales, treatises, political pamphlets, have been largely ignored by commentators; it is on the above books that Sade's reputation as a pornographer rests.

He was unusual in his period for claiming rights of free sexuality for women, and in installing women as beings of power in his imaginary worlds. This sets him apart from all other pornographers at all times and most other writers of his period.

In the looking-glass of Sade's misanthropy, women may see themselves as they have been and it is an uncomfortable sight. He offers an extraordinary variety of male fantasies about women and, because of the equivocal nature of his own sexual response, a number of startling insights. His misanthropy bred a hatred of the mothering function that led him to demystify the most sanctified aspects of women and if he invented women who suffered, he also invented women who caused suffering. The hole the pornographer Sade leaves in his text is just sufficient for a flaying; for a castration. It is a hole large enough for women to see themselves as if the fringed hole of graffiti were a spyhole into territory that had been forbidden them.

This book, which takes as its starting point of cultural exploration the wealth of philosophically pornographic material about women that Sade provides, is an exercise of the lateral imagination. Sade remains a monstrous and daunting cultural edifice; yet I would like to think that he put pornography in the service of women, or, perhaps, allowed it to be invaded by an ideology not inimical to women. And give the old monster his due; let us introduce him with an exhilarating burst of rhetoric:

Charming sex, you will be free: just as men do, you shall enjoy all the pleasures that Nature makes your duty, do not withold yourselves from one. Must the more divine half of mankind be kept in chains by the others? Ah, break those bonds: nature wills it.

TWO

The Desecration of the Temple:
The Life of Justine

All the idealisations of the female from the earliest days of
courtly love have been in fact devices to deprive her of freedom
and self-determination.

> *Love and Death in the American Novel,*
> Leslie Fiedler

*Dans le sacrifice, la victime était choisie de telle manière que sa per-
fection achevat de render sensible la brutalité de la mort.*
> *L'Erotisme,* Georges Bataille

. . . it's so different a life from what all girls expect.
> Letter quoted from a woman seeking birth control in
> *Motherhood in Bondage,* Margaret Sanger

I ANGEL-FACE ON THE RUN

Justine is a good woman in a man's world. She is a good woman
according to the rules for women laid down by men and her reward
is rape, humiliation and incessant beatings. Her life is that of a
woman martyrised by the circumstances of her life as a woman.

The Justine of *Justine, or The Misfortunes of Virtue*, edition of 1791, is a beautiful and penniless orphan, the living image of a fairy-tale princess in disguise but a Cinderella for whom the ashes with which she is covered have become part of the skin. She rejects the approaches of a fairy godmother because the woman is a criminal; she falls in love, not with a handsome prince, but with a murderous homosexual who sets his dogs upon her and frames her for a murder he has himself committed. So she is the heroine of a black, inverted fairy tale and its subject is the misfortunes of unfreedom; Justine embarks on a dolorous pilgrimage in which each proffered sanctuary turns out to be a new prison and all the human relations offered her are a form of servitude.

The recurring images of the novel are the road, the place of flight and hence of momentary safety; the forest, the place of rape; and the fortress, the place of confinement and pain. She is always free only in the act of escape for the road down which she perpetually flees is, in spite of its perils, always a safer place than the refuges she spies with such relief, that offer her only pain, humiliation and a gross genital acting-out of the hatred of men for the women whose manners they have invented, and related to this, of the pure and impersonal hatred of the strong for the weak.

Always the object of punishment, she has committed only one crime and that was an involuntary one; she was born a woman, and, for that, she is ceaselessly punished. The innocent girl pays a high price for the original if imaginary crime of Eve, just as Saint Paul said she should, and her protracted and exemplary Calvary makes her a female Christ whom a stern and patriarchal god has by no means forsaken but takes an especial delight in tormenting. Our revulsion at this spectacle is not unrelated to the uncomfortable truths it contains.

But there is no mysterious virtue in Justine's suffering. The martyrdom of this Christ-figure is absolutely useless; she is a gratuitous victim. And if there is no virtue in her suffering, then there is none, it turns out, in her virtue itself; it does nobody any good, least of all herself.

Justine is first introduced to the reader almost at the end of her unfortunate career, swathed to the eyes in a black cloak, bound securely hand and foot, a parcel of bereft humanity on its way to the gallows. This pathetic bundle is handed down unceremoniously from the roof of a carriage by a detachment of policemen at a coach stop and she narrates her life from its beginnings to a pair of sympathetic listeners, the first sympathy she has encountered for years.

Left penniless when her parents died of grief on becoming bankrupt, Justine's first lesson in life is that of the indignities of poverty. Those to whom her parents had been charitable drive her from their doors; the landlady of the garret in which she lives berates her for refusing to sell herself to a rich gentleman – does Justine think men are such fools as to give something for nothing to little girls like herself? A woman on her own must learn to give men pleasure for that is the only way she can earn a living; but Justine cannot bring herself to put an exchange value on her body, only on her labour, and so obtains a post as maid of all work in the house of the usurer, du Harpin, where she must not dust the furniture for fear of wearing it out. This is her first experience of wage-labour and terminates when she refuses to rob a neighbour on du Harpin's instructions. He has her arrested on a false charge and, because she is poor, friendless and a woman, she cannot obtain a hearing and is condemned to death.

In prison, awaiting execution, she meets a woman who offers herself as a surrogate mother and instructress in the ways of the world, the brigand chieftainess, La Dubois, who has also been condemned to death. When La Dubois's confederates set fire to the prison, she and Justine escape together. La Dubois assures Justine that the practice of virtue will have her on the dung heap in no time. Like Bakunin, La Dubois suggests that the callousness of the rich justifies the crimes of the poor and asks Justine to join the robber band, but Justine, though almost persuaded by La Dubois's arguments, decides she will never fall from virtue. The robbers offer Justine a life that is not a form of slavery although, or because, it is that of the outlaw. The law itself has already shown Justine it will give her no protection but she cannot persuade herself to commit a transgression against the law. To live outside the law is to live in exile from the communities of humanity. She cannot do that because she is not inhuman, even though the law is not just. Her poverty, her weakness, her femaleness and her goodness put her on the wrong side of the law already but her dilemma is this; she has done nothing wrong.

Coeur-de-Fer, Heart-of-Iron, La Dubois's senior henchman, suggests that her virtue does not necessarily depend on the greater or lesser diameter of her vagina; at this stage, Justine is still a virgin. This is today a suggestion less radical than it was in the eighteenth century. But Justine refuses to sleep with him and takes the first opportunity that presents itself to flee the robber camp with a captive the band has just taken, Saint-Florent. For this desertion, La Dubois will later hound her like a fury, like a mother whose child has betrayed her – and La Dubois did indeed offer Justine a kind of mothering.

As soon as they reach the forest, Saint-Florent rapes Justine, robs her and leaves her alone and half-naked. Waking from a faint, she sees a valet buggering the Count de Bressac and overhears them plotting the death of de Bressac's rich aunt. They capture Justine, torture her and take her home, where de Bressac's aunt employs her as a chambermaid, out of charity. De Bressac threatens to murder Justine if she reveals his plot; she falls in love with him, in spite of his aversion to women. At last, he asks her to poison his aunt for him and at first she refuses, then pretends to agree, meanwhile informing his aunt. Discovering Justine's betrayal, de Bressac poisons his aunt himself, sets his dogs upon Justine and leaves her with the information that she is still wanted by the police for the robbery from du Harpin and also for causing the fire that released her from prison in the first place. He adds to her impressive if entirely fictitious criminal record the murder of his aunt, of which he has accused her.

Justine now takes refuge with an atheist surgeon, Rodin, and Rodin's daughter, Rosalie, whom her father had seduced when she was eleven years old. Rodin unsuccessfully attempts to seduce Justine, who consents to remain in the house as Rosalie's companion, with the secret plan of accomplishing Rosalie's conversion to Christianity. She succeeds in doing this shortly before Rodin locks his daughter up in the cellar as a preparation for her murder; he proposes to perform a scientific dissection upon her. Justine unlocks the cellar door but she and Rosalie are discovered before they can escape. Rodin is incensed Justine should try to abduct a daughter from her father's care and has her branded on the shoulder. This branding defines Justine as a common criminal. She wears her punishment on her skin, although she has not committed a single crime. Then he leaves her weeping in the forest.

She travels on until she sees the spire of the monastery of St Mary-in-the-Wood among the trees and decides to spend a few days there, tasting the solaces of religion.

The monastery of St Mary-in-the-Wood is the novel's largest set-piece, a microcosm in which a small group of privileged men operate a system of government by terror upon a seraglio of kidnapped women. As in all the Sadeian places of confinement, intimidation alone prevails and the only reward of virtue is to escape punishment, while virtue, as in the nursery, consists solely in observing an arbitrary set of rules. The monastery is utterly isolated; attached to the church is a secret pleasure pavilion, lavishly funded by the Benedictine order, whose notables have the right of residence here.

Brought here by force, their girls are released from the pavilion only by death. It is as if the place of terror and of privilege is a model of the world; we don't ask to come here and may leave it only once. Our entrance and our exit is alike violent and involuntary; choice has nothing to do with it. But our residence within this confinement is not upon equal terms.

The task of the girls is to minister to the pleasures of their masters, the monks. Complete submissiveness is their only lot. When a new girl is brought into the community, one of the residents is selected at random for 'retirement', that is, murder. The girls, all beautiful, all well-born, wear uniforms according to age groups; their lives are governed by a rigid system of regulations which exist primarily to provide the monks innumerable opportunities for punishment. Disordered hair, twenty strokes of the whip; getting up late in the morning, thirty strokes of the whip; pregnancy, a hundred strokes of the whip. The girls have no personal property. There is no privacy, except in the lavatory. For us, there is no hope at all. The monks rule their little world with the whim of oligarchs, of fate or of God. It is oddly like a British public school. It is like all hierarchical institutions.

With a pretty wit, the Benedictines have named their retreat after the Holy Virgin, and sited it deep in the heart of the forest, the place of rape. In this pleasure pavilion, the pleasure of a small minority of men devolves upon the pain of the majority, their serving women. Here, professional celibates extort unpaid sexual labour from sixteen well-trained women; these women are reduced entirely to their sexual function. Apart from that, they are nothing. There is a suggestion, made, rather touchingly, by the monk Clement, that these young and lovely women would never dream of performing such services for the ugly old men if they were not forced to do so. (Sade can never understand why women should wish to engage in sexual activity with ugly old men; he finds it perverse. They must do it from fear or for profit, he reasons. What *pleasure* can there be in it for them? It puzzles him very much.)

The sexual function of the women in the monastery is a thorough negation of their existence as human beings. Justine is told she is as good as dead as soon as she enters the monastery. But Justine has a phenomenal resilience; shortly after her friend, Omphale, has been 'retired', Justine escapes by sawing through the bars on her dressing-room window and cutting through the thick hedge that surrounds the monastery. She prays to be forgiven the sins she has unwillingly committed at the hands of the monks and sets out on the road to Dijon.

She is immediately captured by the servants of the Count de Gernande and taken to his lonely chateau, to serve as his wife's maid. If the monastery was an oligarchy, then de Gernande's house is an absolute dictatorship. De Gernande metaphorically bleeds his tenants white; he is literally bleeding his wife to death, to satisfy his fetish for blood. To conceal this crime, he has told his wife's mother that the woman has gone mad and must not be visited. Gernande's life is all of a piece and self-consistent. Like a good vampire, it is the physical energy of the woman he extracts; he is a monstrously fat man, he has grown fat on the substance of his wives, for this is not the first woman he has killed in such a way.

Justine offers to take a letter to the Countess's mother and escapes from the house only to find herself in a walled garden. The count discovers her. She throws herself on his mercy and asks him to punish her. She fails to conceal the Countess's letter and he reads it. He imprisons Justine in a dungeon but, excited by the news his wife is now dying, he forgets to lock the door and Justine flees.

She takes the road to Grenoble, where she re-encounters Saint-Florent, who originally deflowered her. He offers her the post of his procuress, which she refuses, and continues south. A beggar asks for alms, as a ruse; Justine is once again robbed but, finding a man who has been robbed and also severely beaten, she cares for him, consoling herself with the reflection that his condition is worse than hers. When he recovers, he offers her a post as his sister's maid – charity disguised as servitude, again – and Justine goes off to the mountains with Roland the counterfeiter.

Roland exploits women primarily as labour but, like Justine's other masters, he enjoys the simple fact of mastery over her most of all. At his castle, with the secret torture chamber in its cellarage, she is lashed to a wheel with four other naked women; draws water; breaks stones; is beaten and forced to take part in Roland's cruel game of 'cut-the-cord'.

The game of 'cut-the-cord' involves the hanging of a girl. The rope is cut, at the last moment, after Roland has enjoyed the spectacle of her terror, but, when Justine's friend, Suzanne, plays 'cut-the-cord', Roland does not cut the rope. Because Justine is so virtuous, Roland trusts her and invites her to cut the rope when he himself plays the game; he likes to play games with death himself, as well as watching them. She is tempted to let him hang but virtue asserts itself and she cuts the rope. He rewards her by suspending her in a pit filled with decomposing corpses. He departs for Italy, leaving the care of the castle in the hands of a kinder governor. In his absence, the castle is stormed by the police and those within it arrested. The kind caretaker will pay for the crimes of his master.

A magistrate interests himself in Justine's case and obtains her release. The rest are hung. In the inn where she lodges, she meets again the brigand chieftainess, La Dubois, who has become very rich by the practice of crime. La Dubois asks Justine to rob Dubreuil, a young man who has fallen in love with Justine. She prevents the robbery and accepts Dubreuil's offer of marriage, only to find that La Dubois has already poisoned him. He dies. La Dubois has already incriminated Justine for his death and left the town. A friend of Dubreuil's suggests Justine should run away too, and secures her a place travelling to the provinces with a Madame Bertrand and her child. Before they can set off, La Dubois, intent on vengeance, kidnaps Justine and delivers her to a local libertine but La Dubois and this cruel gentleman drink too much and fall asleep so Justine once again escapes.

She sets off with Madame Bertrand and the child but La Dubois, an avenging angel, sets fire to the hotel in which they spend the night and the child dies. La Dubois seizes Justine and is whisking her off for punishment when the police stop them and arrest Justine for an immense list of offences culminating in the burning of the hotel and the murder of the baby. La Dubois gladly gives Justine up to the law, which is as arbitrary and despotic as any of her other masters.

In prison, she begs aid from several of her former tormentors and all refuse, although Saint-Florent takes her out of the prison for an orgy, in which the judge also participates. Justine's reluctance ensures she will be found guilty at her trial.

She is on her way to her execution when she recounts this sad life to the rich lady and gentleman at the coach stop. The weeping and astonished lady now reveals herself as Justine's long-lost sister, Juliette, who, when their parents died, did not beg for charity at all but immediately apprenticed herself to a brothel and has done very well for herself. Her lover, a Councillor to the State, obtains Justine's release. She is taken to their sumptuous house and cared for while her name is cleared in the courts. A surgeon removes the brand from her shoulder; none of her tribulations has left her with a permanent stain. All goes well for Justine at last but she cannot believe the good times will last for ever and, one stormy summer's evening, she is struck through the heart by a thunderbolt and so dies.

Juliette and her lover are overwhelmed with grief and remorse. Juliette enters a convent and devotes the rest of her life to good works. This devotional conclusion is amended in the sequel to this novel.

Justine's pilgrimage consists of the road; the forest; and the place of confinement. Nowhere is she safe from abuse. Upon her lovely and innocent head fall an endless stream of the ghastliest misfortunes and her virtue, the passive virtue of a good woman, ensures she can never escape them because the essence of her virtue is doing what she is told. Yet she is also trusting, endlessly trusting, ruled by ingenuousness, candour and guilelessness, a heroine out of Jean-Jacques Rousseau; she possesses all the limpid innocence he admired in children and savages yet when she offers this innocence to others as shyly as if she were offering a bunch of flowers, it is trampled in the mud. She is a selfless heroine of Rousseau in the egocentric and cruel world of Hobbes.

It is a matter for discussion as to how far Justine's behaviour is innately that of a woman or how far she has adopted the stance of the cringe as a means of self-defence. She is not only a woman in a man's world; she is also a receptacle of feeling, a repository of the type of sensibility we call 'feminine'.

Her very first adventure is an emotional model for all the others. Justine is nothing if not self-conscious in her innocence and knows how to make a touching picture out of her misfortunes. She goes to seek help from the family priest, pale with mourning, tear-stained, in a little white dress, with that unshelled vulnerability of all literary orphans of whom she herself is both the apogee and the prototype. She presents herself emblematically in the passive mood, as an object of pity and as a suppliant. The priest tries to kiss her. She reprimands him; she is driven with blows and abuse from his door.

The question of her virtue is itself an interesting one. As the brigand, Coeur-de-Fer, says to her: why does such an intelligent girl so persistently locate virtue in the region of her genitals?

For Justine's conception of virtue is a specifically feminine one in that sexual abstinence plays a large part in it. In common speech, a 'bad boy' may be a thief, or a drunkard, or a liar, and not necessarily just a womaniser. But a 'bad girl' always contains the meaning of a sexually active girl and Justine knows she is good because she does not fuck. When, against her will, she *is* fucked, she knows she remains good because she does not feel pleasure. She implores La Dubois's brigands to spare her honour, that is, to refrain from deflowering her; a woman's honour, in the eighteenth century, is always a matter of her sexual reputation. Obeying the letter if not the spirit of her request, they strip her, sexually abuse her and ejaculate upon her body. 'They respected my honour, if not my modesty,' she congratulates herself. Her virginity has a metaphysical import-ance to her. Her unruptured hymen is a visible sign of her purity, even if her breasts and belly have been deluged in spunk.

Later, her virginity gone, she will tell herself that she has nothing to reproach herself with but a rape and, since that was involuntary, it was not a sin. She is less scrupulous than her lit-erary progenitor, Richardson's Clarissa Harlowe, the first great suffering virgin in the history of literature, who, though she had been drugged into unconsciousness while the act took place, still believed herself in complicity with a rape of which she had known nothing. Justine is less scrupulous because her virtue is a female ruse that denies her own sexuality; nevertheless, though she may deplore the sexuality of incontinent men who think of rape the moment they see her, as all men do with Justine, she is sufficiently pragmatic to have deduced, from the fact that rape has patently not changed her, that Coeur-de-Fer was right and virtue does not depend exclusively on the state of her hymen. She concludes her virtue depends on her own reluctance.

Her sexual abstinence, her denial of her own sexuality, is what makes her important to herself. Her passionately held conviction that her morality is intimately connected with her genitalia makes it become so. Her honour does indeed reside in her vagina because she honestly believes it does so. She has seized on the only area she is certain of as a means of nourishing her own self-respect, even if it involves the cruellest repressions and a good deal of physical distress.

Repression is Justine's whole being – repression of sex, of anger and of her own violence; the repressions demanded of Christian virtue, in fact. She cannot conceive of any pleasure at all in the responses of her own body to sexual activity, and so automatically precludes the possibility of accidentally experiencing pleasure.

Justine is the broken heart, the stabbed dove, the violated sepulchre, the persecuted maiden whose virginity is perpetually refreshed by rape. She will never feel one moment's gratification in any of her numerous, diverse and involuntary erotic encounters; she mimics sexual pleasure to ingratiate herself with the chief wardress of the girls at the monastery of St Mary-in-the-Wood but in reality assures us she felt nothing, as if, now she is no longer a virgin, her chastity can still exist in the form of frigidity. She seems almost a monster of the fear of sexuality.

Since she herself denies the violence of her own desires, all her sexual encounters become for her a form of violence because she is not free to judge them. The fluids of *her* orgasm are the tears that are an implicit invitation to further rapes. For she does not fear rape at all; it is over in a moment and implies no relation with the aggressor. The violent but brief mastery of rape leaves her sense of self inviolate. A rape may be performed in the singular and denies the notion of consent. It is not rape but seduction she fears, and the loss of self in participating in her own seduction, for one must be willing or deluded, or, at least, willing to be deluded, in order to be seduced.

When she is offered seduction by the outlaws, she instinctively rejects it. It is not only that she senses the snare in this first seduction, that it will lead to her prostitution. But she cannot envisage a benign sexuality and, though her strength lies in her refusal to do so, nevertheless, the limitations of her sexuality are the limitations of her life. She sees herself only as the object of lust. She does not act, she is. She is the object of a thousand different passions, some of them very strange, but she is the subject of not a single one. She can indulge in her infatuation for the homosexual de Bressac because she knows in advance he will be indifferent to her. Later, she accepts Dubreuil's proposal of marriage solely because he has made it to her; it is not the exercise of a choice and, besides, her own sexual response does not enter into the contractual obligations of marriage.

But she has done nothing at all to deserve the pain inflicted upon her except to juxtapose the expectations of a well brought-up virgin, daughter of a rich banker, against the harsh cynicism of poverty. The rich can afford to be virtuous, the poor must shift as best they can. Justine's femininity is a mode of behaviour open only to those who can afford it and the price she has to pay for resolutely, indeed heroically maintaining her role of bourgeois virgin against all odds is a solitary confinement in the prison of her own femininity, a solitude alleviated only by the frequent visits of her torturers.

If her suffering itself becomes a kind of mastery, it is a masochistic mastery over herself. Like Patient Grizelda, as if Justine had been the good wife of an ungrateful world, her patience at last exhausts the ingenuity of her torturers, although it is a negative triumph, for though the world will not allow her to earn an honest living – in Sade's version of the world, there is no such thing as an honest living – it permits her to earn her death. In a final act of servitude, she is closing the windows for her sister to keep out the storm when the thunderbolt breaks through the glass and transfixes her.

Her life is dominated by chance, the chance enounters on the road, the chance escapes from prison, the chance thunderbolt. By chance, she passes from the cruel hands of one master to another and her innocence is so perfect that it precludes any advance knowledge of the strength and malice of her adversaries. Justine's life was doomed to disappointment before it began, like that of a woman who wishes for nothing better than a happy marriage. She pins her hopes always on those contingent to her, on the hypothetical benefactor who will protect her; but she meets only brigands, procuresses, woman-haters and rapists and, from these adventures, she learns not self-preservation but self-pity.

She is not in control of her life; her poverty and her femininity conspire to rob her of autonomy. She is always the dupe of an experience that she never experiences *as* experience; her innocence invalidates experience and turns it into events, things that happen to her but do not change her. This is the common experience of most women's lives, conducted always in the invisible presence of others who extract the meaning of her experience for themselves and thereby diminish all meaning, so that a seduction, or a birth, or a marriage, the central events in the lives of most women, the stages of a life, are marginal occurrences in the life of the seducer, the father or the husband.

And Justine's inability to be changed by experience is symbolised by her sterility. Her failure to conceive during ten years of enforced sexual activity is an aspect of her perennial virginity, but it is both a negative and a positive quality at the same time. Rape is unable to modify her intransigent singularity in any way. She is a free woman, in spite of herself.

But she has had her freedom thrust upon her, she has not seized it for herself. Her freedom is as involuntary as her punishment. Her freedom *is* her punishment, in the terms of the idealisation of femininity she represents. She is a caged and cherished bird all at once set free in the dangerous forest and it is a wonder she comes to no worse harm.

Justine's organ of perception is the heart that forbids her to engage in certain activities she feels to be immoral and her autobiography illustrates the moral limitations of a life conducted solely according to the virtuous promptings of the heart. This heart is an organ of sentiment, not of analysis, and it never prompts her to sacrifice herself for the principles by which she claims to live.

In the service of the vampiric Count de Gernande, she is

overcome with pity for the wife he tortures. Nevertheless, when the Count orders her to undress the unfortunate woman and bring her to him, Justine says: 'In spite of the loathing I sensed for all these horrors . . . I had no choice but to submit with the most utmost resignation.' She has no choice because, if she does not do so, she herself will be punished and she cannot imagine how she might purchase Madame de Gernande a brief respite from pain at the price of undergoing a little pain herself.

Her heart is immoderate and if it does not allow her to put an exchange value on her flesh, neither does it allow her to put an exchange value on her suffering. It is a thing-in-itself, perceived as part of her condition. So Justine resolutely eschews the purchasing power of self-sacrifice; there *has* been a choice. Justine could have said 'no' to the Count de Gernande and refused to be his accomplice. But she does not do so. It does not occur to her to do so. She has no sense of identification with other people in pain.

The heart's egoism sees itself suffering when it sees another suffering and so it learns sympathy, because it can put itself in another's place; then the heart comes a little way out of its egoism and tentatively encounters the world. But, before the prospect of its own suffering, the heart melts completely and retreats into egoism, again, to protect itself.

In Gernande's house, Justine's sympathy only succeeds in worsening Madame de Gernande's plight, and her own. She runs away with a letter for Madame de Gernande's mother, whom the women hope will come and rescue them when she receives it. Gernande spies her early in the morning, as she escapes through the garden, just as God caught Adam in the garden on the morning of the primal transgression against authority. But Gernande thinks the girl is a ghost. Like all Sade's libertines, Gernande is a great coward; he is terrified, alone and helpless, and he would be entirely at Justine's mercy had she not quavered, even before he recognised her, 'O, master, punish me.' She demands punishment even before she has been accused. She does not even take advantage of Gernande's confusion to destroy the incriminating letters she carries.

As soon as she asks for punishment, Gernande is reassured. Now he knows who he is; she has told him so, she has told him he is her master. And she has told him what to do to her, to punish her. But he is still not quite sure why he should do it. He suspects Justine must be taking a plea for help to the outside world; he demands the evidence. 'I want to say I do not have it; but Gernande spies the fatal letter protruding above the kerchief at my breast, seizes it, reads it.' She makes no attempt to prevent him doing so. She adopts the humility of the cripple, she is always conciliatory. Her own punishment will be death; though, as she always does, she escapes it. But the punishment of the equally innocent woman she tried to help is an inescapable death. Justine's sympathy is always fatal to its object. Through its own unreason, the heart finds itself in complicity with the morality of cruelty it abhors.

In the castle of the counterfeiter, Roland, Justine is presented with several opportunities of murdering him. Indeed, on one occasion, she could kill him merely by strenuously exercising passivity. He wants her to play his favourite game of 'cut-the-cord'. He proposes to partially hang himself, in order to procure himself a particularly violent orgasm, and it is Justine who must cut the rope at the critical moment, at the point of emission, before death supervenes. He promises her he will set her free if she plays her part well but even Justine does not quite believe that. So Roland puts his life in the hands of a woman he has grievously abused and who has witnessed several of his own murders. Once again, she tells us she had no choice but to act out the part he assigned to her; he is her master and masters exist only in order to be obeyed. She does not even entertain the possibility of murdering him and that is the final limitation of her virtue; the unreason of the heart, the false logic of feeling, forbid her to exert mastery for even one moment and Sade achieves an immoral victory over the reader, who is bound to urge the spotless Justine, just this once, to soil her hands with crime.

Virtue has produced in Justine the same kind of apathy, of insensibility, that criminality has produced in Sade's libertines, who also never concern themselves with the nature of good and evil, who know intuitively what is wrong just as Justine knows intuitively what is right. She is incapable of anger or defiance because of her moral indifference; she feels no anger at the sufferings of her cell mates. She is as much a bourgeois individualist as Roland when she tells us how, during the first game of 'cut-the-cord', she feels an immense sense of happiness and peace when she realises that her companion, Suzanne, is to die and not Justine herself. Her virtue is egocentric, like the vice of the libertines. And it is entirely its own reward.

Indeed, Roland has chosen Justine as a playmate precisely because of the impeccable honesty that will not be seduced for even one treacherous moment by the idea of ridding the world of such a villain as he. He knows how to pick his accomplices. He relies on her native goodness when he puts her in charge of his life; she tells us she takes it into her hands only in order to restore it to him again. Singular generosity, singular magnanimity. If she wavered for a moment when she thought of the dead Suzanne, scarred with the marks of Roland's whips, or of the chain-gang of women who work in the castle, and then did not kill him, her refusal might be glorious; virtue humiliates vice. But Justine does not first judge him and then refuse to pass the death penalty. She exercises the female prerogative of mercy only because she is incapable of judgement and, in that sense, beyond good and evil, just as he is himself. She does not murder Roland only because he asks her not to. 'He is my master and I must obey him.'

Justine's virtue is not the continuous exercise of a moral faculty. It is a sentimental response to a world in which she always hopes her good behaviour will procure her some reward, some respite from the bleak and intransigent reality which surrounds her and to which she cannot accommodate herself. The virtuous, the interesting Justine, with her incompetence, her gullibility, her whining, her frigidity, her reluctance to take control of her own life, is a perfect woman. She always does what she is told. She is at the mercy of any master, because that is the nature of her own definition of goodness.

Her Christian virtues expose the praxis of the world. Her charity is always rewarded by theft; her piety leads her directly to the horrors of St Mary-in-the-Wood; when she converts the daughter of the surgeon, Rodin, to religion, she ensures the girl will die. Justine's virtue, in action, is the liberal lie in action, a good heart and an inadequate methodology.

In a world where women are commodities, a woman who refuses to sell herself will have the thing she refuses to sell taken away from her by force. The piety, the gentleness, the honesty, the sensitivity, all the qualities she has learned to admire in herself, are invitations to violence; all her life, she has been groomed for the slaughterhouse. And though she is virtuous, she does not know how to do good.

It is easy for a child to be good; a child's goodness is a negative quality. He is good if he does not do anything bad. A grown-up, however, cannot get away with this docile passivity. He must act out his virtue amongst an audience of others that includes himself. Doing good implies a social context of action, a whole system of social relations and Justine has been involuntarily deprived of this system. She does not even know it exists. She is a child who knows how to be good to please daddy; but the existence of daddy, her god, the abstract virtue to which she constantly refers, prevents her from acting for herself.

Nevertheless, her foolish and ignorant heart is never corrupted. The masters seek, always, not the submission of her body; that is easy for her to give, she always submits her flesh without any fuss – but they do not really want that. They want the submission of her heart and that she will never give. Good behaviour is always well chastised but never converted into its own opposite. The victim is always morally superior to the master; that is the victim's ambivalent triumph. That is why there have been so few notoriously wicked women in comparison to the number of notoriously wicked men; our victim status ensures that we rarely have the opportunity. Virtue is thrust upon us. If that is nothing, in itself, to be proud of, at least it is nothing of which to be ashamed.

So evil, the desire for dominance, gains a Pyrrhic victory

over Justine, in the destruction but never the surrender of the object on which it vents its rage. 'The fool who persists in his folly becomes wise,' says Blake. In its fatal *single-mindedness*, Justine's negative capability for virtue becomes an involuntary affirmation of the humanism that the world in which she lives denies, even if not an affirmation of her own positive humanity, for that exists by accident.

Flight is Justine's salvation. She is woman as an escape artist, for whom only the self-defining life of the traveller, all of whose homes are aspects of a perpetual homelessness, offers freedom from the definitions of servitude that are all her female virtue is offered. And she must die an emotional, if not a physical virgin, like her literary granddaughters, Beth in *Little Women*, Eva in *Uncle Tom's Cabin*, the little girls who died in the angelic state of pre-pubescence and go straight to heaven, to daddy, because they are too good to live. This good little girl's martyrisation by the circumstances of adult life as a woman makes her the ancestress of a generation of women in popular fiction who find themselves in the same predicament, such as the heart-struck, tearful heroines of Jean Rhys, Edna O'Brien and Joan Didion who remain grumblingly acquiescent in a fate over which they believe they have no control. By some accident of literature, the unfortunate heroine of Judith Rossner's best-selling piece of didactic soft-core pornography, *Looking For Mr Goodbar*, even has the same name, Teresa, that Justine uses in disguise. There is presumably no direct literary influence from the eighteenth-century philosophical pornographer to these contemporary women novelists; but, in the character of Justine, Sade contrived to isolate the dilemma of an emergent type of woman. Justine, daughter of a banker, becomes the prototype of two centuries of women who find the world was not, as they had been promised, made for them and who do not have, because they have not been given, the existential tools to remake the world for themselves. These self-consciously blameless ones suffer and suffer until it becomes second nature; Justine marks the start of a kind of self-regarding female masochism, a woman with no place in the world, no status, the core of whose resistance has been eaten away by self-pity.

Justine's place in the aetiology of the female condition in the twentieth century is assured; she is the personification of the pornography of that condition.

She is obscene to the extent to which she is beautiful. Her beauty, her submissiveness and the false expectations that these qualities will do her some good are what make her obscene.

II THE BLONDE AS CLOWN

The real value of a sexually attractive woman in a world which regards good looks as a commodity depends on the degree to which she puts her looks to work for her. The lovely Justine, the sacred woman, denies her value in this world by refusing to sell herself on any terms and even refusing to accept the notion of the morality of contract. But her body is by far the most valuable thing she has to sell. She will never make a living out of the sale of her labour power, alone.

However, in a world organised by contractual obligations, the whore represents the only possible type of honest woman. If the world in its present state is indeed a brothel – and the moral difference between selling one's sexual labour and one's manual labour is, in these terms, though never in Justine's terms, an academic one – then every attempt the individual makes to escape the conditions of sale will only bring a girl back to the crib, again, in some form or another. At least the girl who sells herself with her eyes open is not a hypocrite and, in a world with a cash-sale ideology, that is a positive, even a heroic virtue.

The whore has made of herself her own capital investment. Her product – her sexual activity, her fictitious response – is worth precisely what the customer is willing to pay for it, no more and no less, but that is only what is true of all products. But the whore is depised by the hypocritical world because she has made a realistic assessment of her assets and does not have to rely on fraud to make a living. In an area of human relations where fraud is regular practice between the sexes, her honesty is regarded with a mocking wonder. She sells herself; but she is a fair tradesman and her explicit acceptance of contractual obligation implicit in all sexual relations mocks the fraud of the 'honest' woman who will give nothing at all in return for goods and money except the intangible and hence unassessable perfume of her presence. The honest whore is assured of her own immediate value, not only in her own valuation but in the valuation of her customers. So she can afford to ignore the opinion of the rest of the world but she will not be respected for her integrity although, if she is successful enough, and her business prospers, she may 'ruin' men, like any other successful entrepreneur.

Justine's profane sister, Juliette, has 'ruined' a number of rich men by the time she meets and succours her wretched sister, even in the relatively decorous pages of the *Justine* of 1791. At this period, 'ruin', applied to a man, means financial ruin, whereas, applied to a woman, it means only that a woman has engaged in sexual activity, suggesting an actual parallel between a bank balance and a body. A ruined woman is one who has lost her capital assets, a virgin who has been deflowered and hence has nothing tangible to put on the market. Not a woman's face but her unruptured hymen is her fortune; however, if she regards her sexual activity as her capital, she may, once ruined, utilise her vagina to ruin others, as though, in fact, the opening of it allowed her access to a capital sum which had been frozen by virginity. No longer a virgin, she may put her capital to work for her.

A businessman in the same position as a successful whore would be applauded for his acumen and admired for his ruthlessness. The woman is censured for her immoral rapacity, although it is the same thing.

But the woman who makes no bones about selling herself will soon adopt the ideology of the small shopkeeper and identify her interests with the status quo. She will be a great upholder of marriage; doesn't the greater part of her trade come from married men? By accepting the contractual nature of sexual relations, even if on her own terms, she imprisons herself within them just as securely as a wife does, though she may retain a greater degree of individual independence. If marriage is legalised prostitution, then prostitution is itself a form of group marriage.

However, the whore may recoup some of the moral status she lost when she sold herself if she concludes her career by 'throwing herself away'. A woman who throws herself away is one who forms arbitrary sexual relations without any thought for their consequences. She will be regarded, not so much as pitiable, though she may condescendingly be pitied; rather, as feckless. The tart with a heart of gold, a mercantile image, is a tart who fecklessly gives away a substance that is as good as money. If physical generosity in a woman is reprehensible when used as a means of financial gain, it is clearly incomprehensible if it is spontaneous. 'Beauty too rich for use, for earth too dear'; a beautiful woman as such is so much bric-a-brac, and all her use value, that is, her sexual value, is denied her.

In the celluloid brothel of the cinema, where the merchandise may be eyed endlessly but never purchased, the tension between the beauty of women, which is admirable, and the denial of the sexuality which is the source of that beauty but is also immoral, reaches a perfect impasse. That is why Saint Justine became the patroness of the screen heroine.

The first attempt to get out of this predicament, that of the moral irreconcilability of physical attractiveness and sexuality, was the invention of the pre-sexual waif as heroine, a role Mary Pickford played until the brink of middle age. Sometimes this waif, as in Griffiths' *Broken Blossoms*, is as innocently erotic and as hideously martyrised as Justine herself, and, as a sexual icon, the abused waif allowed the customer to have his cake and glut himself upon it, too. She could be as enticing in her vulnerability and ringletted prettiness as she was able but the audience knew all the time that the lovely child before them was, in fact, a mature woman whom the fiction of her childishness made taboo. The taboo against acknowledging her sexuality created the convention that the child could not arouse desire; if she did so, it was denied. A sentimental transformation turned the denial of lust into a kitsch admiration of the 'cute'.

The taboo on the sexuality of the pre-pubescent child, who

is tacitly assumed to be sexually inactive, also extends to the defusing of the potential menace of the sexuality of the middle-aged woman, whose sexual life may be assumed to be at an end. Mae West's sexuality, the most overt in the history of the cinema, could only be tolerated on the screen because she did not arrive in Hollywood until she had reached the age associated with menopause. This allowed her some of the anarchic freedom of the female impersonator, pantomime dame, who is licensed to make sexual innuendos because his masculinity renders them a form of male aggression upon the women he personates.

Mae West's joke upon her audience was, however, a superior kind of double bluff. She was in reality a sexually free woman, economically independent, who wrote her own starring vehicles in her early days in the theatre and subsequently exercised an iron hand on her own Hollywood career. The words she spoke in her movies were the words she had written herself; the dramatised version of herself she presented to the world was based on the one she both invented and lived for herself. Age did not wither her but only increased her self-confidence until she could actually pretend to be a female impersonator, aided, not desexualised, by the maturity which frees women of the fecundity which is the most troubling aspect of their sexuality. If Mae West has a Sadeian avatar, it is neither Justine nor Juliette but the sterile, phallic mother who will succour not Justine but Juliette and teach Eugénie de Mistival the philosophy of the boudoir. Mae West's wit is castratory, if tender; and the part of her mind which is not scheming for libidinal gratification is adding up her bank accounts.

She selected theatrical and cinematic roles of women whose

work entailed sexual self-display yet her ability to act out these roles on the screen was due solely to her middle-age, even if she was permitted to do so because she did not look middle-aged. She was forty when she made her first film in Hollywood, *Night after Night*, in 1932. The middle-aged woman, whose literary prototype is the nurse in *Romeo and Juliet*, may say what she pleases, wink at and nudge whomever she desires but we know it is all a joke upon her, for she is licensed to be free because she is so old and ugly that nobody will have her. Mae West relied on this freedom, even if she turned it on its head; universally desired, absolutely her own woman, she could pick and choose among her adorers with the cynical facility of the rake, inverting the myth of female masochism even in the titles of her movies – *She Done Him Wrong*, 1933. She made of her own predatoriness a joke that concealed its power, whilst simultaneously exploiting it. Yet she represents a sardonic disregard of convention rather than a heroic overthrow of taboo.

The European love-goddesses, Garbo and Dietrich, were another story. They brought their foreignness to Hollywood with them; to the country where girls learned the techniques of self-effacement from books called *Little Women* and *Good Wives*, they arrived fully fledged from Europe, the domain of adultery, where the fulfilled sexuality of women was culturally admitted and its socially disruptive quality acknowledged, even if it was always given a tragic resonance in the mythology of doomed adultery implicit in Flaubert's *Madame Bovary*, Tolstoy's *Anna Karenina*. If a tragic resonance to illicit fuckery is as silly as a straightforward denial that it exists, then at least it gives illicit fuckery a silly kind of dignity, and the adulteress can retain a little self-respect. Besides, the adulteress, if she plays her cards right, may evolve into the adventuress, whose status in life, if not in art, has always been that of a free woman.

Garbo and Dietrich both retained the air of the European adventuress. However discreetly they behaved in life – and both were models of discretion – it was obvious that their screen personalities had a stock-in-trade that consisted of more than an unruptured hymen. Besides, both often appeared in drag, which is always reassuring to men, since a woman who pretends to be a man has also cancelled out her reproductive system, like the post-menopausal woman, and may also freely function as a safety valve for homoerotic fantasy.

The public sexual ideology of Hollywood finally formulated itself, in the nineteen forties, as a version of Justine's own. Female virtue was equated with frigidity and a woman's morality with her sexual practice. (These equations neatly deny women any access to questions of public morality.)

But, of course, it proved quite impossible to keep sexuality off the screen. It consistently reasserted itself, even when female virtue was equated with asexuality, because a pretty face and a provocative body remained the first prerequisites of success for a woman in the movies. The movies celebrated allure in itself but either denied the attractions inherent in availability or treated availability itself as a poor joke.

The cultural product of this tension was the Good Bad Girl, the blonde, buxom and unfortunate sorority of Saint Justine, whose most notable martyr is Marilyn Monroe.

See how alike they look! Marilyn Monroe, the living image of Justine; both have huge, appealing, eloquent eyes, the open windows of the soul; their dazzling fair skins are of such a delicate texture that they look as if they will bruise at a touch, carrying the exciting stigmata of sexual violence for a long time, and that is why gentlemen prefer blondes. Marilyn/Justine has a childlike candour and trust and there is a faint touch of melancholy about her that has been produced by this trust, which is always absolute and always betrayed. This quality of trust is what the Sadeian libertines find most fascinating of all. Connoisseurs of the poetry of masochism that they are, they immediately recognise those girls who will look most beautiful when they are crying. Saint Fond, who employs Justine's wicked, brunette sister, Juliette, as his procuress, questions her anxiously about one of her finds: 'Does she weep? I love to see women weep; with me, they always do, all of them.'

The essence of the physicality of the most famous blonde in the world is a wholesome eroticism blurred a little round the edges by the fact that she herself is not quite sure what eroticism is. This gives her her tentative luminosity and makes her, somehow, always more like her own image in the mirror than she is like herself. To this, she owes her poetic ambiguity and her appearance of fragility. Marilyn Monroe's representative capacity for exquisite martyrdom is so extreme that Norman Mailer's life of her is composed entirely in mythic, rather than factual terms. His biography, *Marilyn, is* a contemporary version of the martyrdom of Justine and, like a hagiography or dirty book, the text has to be helped along with pictures before you can make sense of it. You have to see her to know how she will look in extremis, which is, in your secret heart, the way you want to see her – men; and women, too, who need to convince themselves that the beauty they deny themselves will always cause suffering to its unfortunate possessors. Mailer endows his saint with all the tawdry rhetoric he can muster up about the pathos inherent in prime, blonde flesh. And she has all the dreadful innocence of lack of self-knowledge, too; she is almost a holy fool. Mailer approvingly quotes Diana Trilling:

> None but Marilyn Monroe could suggest such a purity of sexual delight. The boldness with which she could parade herself and yet never be gross, her sexual flamboyance and bravado which yet breathed an air of mystery and reticence, her voice which carried such ripe overtones of erotic excitement and yet was the voice of a tiny child – these complications were integral to her gift. And they described a young woman trapped in some never-never land of unawareness.

This is an apt anthem for Justine, always the unwitting prey, who could have said, just as Monroe said to Groucho Marx in *Monkey Business*: 'Men keep following me all the time', without the least notion why they did so. If she had had the self-confidence to be gross – because what is *wrong* with being gross? – the story would have been quite different.

Marilyn's lonely death by barbiturates, nude, in bed, a death adored and longed for by all necrophiles, is the contemporary death-by-lightning of the sweet, dumb blonde, the blue-eyed lamb with the golden fleece led to slaughter on the altar of the world. You can even see real scar-tissue (from a gall-bladder operation; the female interior bearing the marks of the intimate, cruel excavation of the scalpel) in the nude pictures Bert Stern took of her the summer before her death. Since a child, she had been steeped in the doctrines of Christian Science: 'Divine love has always met and always will meet every human need', the pious Justine's own, unspoken maxim in a novel which is the pilgrimage of the soul in search of god written by an atheist.

Monroe was not born but became a blonde; blondeness is a state of ambivalent grace, to which anyone who wants it badly enough may aspire. According to Fred Lawrence Guiles' biography of her, *Norma Jean*, Monroe's agent told her, in 1946: 'I have a call for a light blonde, honey or platinum.' In this world, women may be ordered like steaks, well-done, medium rare, bloody. The identity of the blonde was the most commercially viable one available; cash betrayed her to sanctity and if she voluntarily took up blondehood, she always voluntarily took upon herself the entire apparatus of the orphan. Fatherless already through illegitimacy, she, heart-struck by the poignancy of her situation, invented for herself a true orphan's biography of hardship, a childhood spent in orphanages where she scrubbed floors, was beaten, accused of theft, bedded down in windowless cupboards and, inevitably, raped.

These misfortunes add the irresistible dew of suffering to her ripeness. 'I see your suffering,' says the hero of Arthur Miller's play, *After the Fall*, to a woman with a scandalous resemblance to Monroe. A visible capacity for suffering provokes further suffering. She is a past master at inspiring rage and at deflecting it from herself on to her entire sex; is she not a sex symbol, and hence the symbolic personification of her entire sex? After *Some Like It Hot* was finished, the director, Billy Wilder, told an interviewer that it had been many weeks before he 'could look at my wife without wanting to hit her because she is a woman'. Mailer lovingly inserts this gossip-column nugget into the myth of 'Marilyn'.

The blonde's physical fragility is, of course, only apparent. She must have a robust constitution to survive the blows life deals her. Her fragility is almost the conscious disguise of masochism and masochism necessitates an infinite resilience. Nevertheless, the victim proclaims her vulnerability in every gesture, every word, every act; defining herself in the third person, the saint laments her lot in *Some Like It Hot*: 'Sugar always gets the fluffy end of the lollipop.' Her misfortunes are no fault of her own, she is quite certain of that; so it is not the demonstration of her innocence itself that makes her innocence real to us. Innocence is a transparent quality, difficult to see in full daylight. Her innocence is made real to us by the desecration of it; the white page is thrown into relief by the spattered mud.

This fatherless and bruisable child was never clever, was dumb; dumb like a fox is dumb, said one of Monroe's lovers. This dumbness is not stupidity but a naivety so perfect it is functionally no different from stupidity; it is only because she is innocent of her own strength that she thinks she will hurt easily. Because she is innocent of her exchange value, she thinks she is valueless.

Monroe, in her major movies, from *Gentlemen Prefer Blondes* to *The Misfits*, is a Good Bad Girl. The theory of the sentimental image of the Good Bad Girl is that she has all the appearance of a tart and an air of continuous availability but, when the chips are down, she would never stoop to sell herself. Less reprehensibly, indeed, almost commendably – and for a moment we are allowed to admire her misguided generosity – she gives it away for free. But her affairs always end badly, her generosity is always abused, she does not realise her flesh is sacred because it is as good as money. In short, she is the most risible and pathetic figure, the unsuccessful prostitute, living proof that crime does not pay and the wages of sin will be too small to pay the rent. Her poor show as a prostitute, as a business woman, is proof in itself that her heart is made of gold.

It is part of Saint Justine's baleful bequest that blonde Good Bad Girls always come to bad ends; brunettes and even redheads, Barbara Stanwyck, Joan Crawford, Shirley Maclaine, have acquired the toughness of Juliette and put their bodies to work actively for them. Indeed, Howard Hawkes' *Gentlemen Prefer Blondes* juxtaposes the deathly fragility of Monroe and the earthiness of Jane Russell almost like a benign version of Sade's diptych.

The mythic role of the Good Bad Girl is, however, directly at variance with the real facts of her life, as all mythic roles are apt to be. She pretends to be an unsuccessful prostitute but, in fact, she is a very successful prostitute indeed and, what is more, one who does not have to deliver the goods. She sells, not the reality of flesh, but its image and so she makes her living, a successful but imaginary prostitute. Yet, since she is not in control of her own marketing, her hypothetical allure and not her actual body is the commodity. She sells a perpetually unfulfilled promise of which the unfulfillment is a consolation rather than a regret. The reality of her could never live up to her publicity. So she retains her theoretical virginity, even if she is raped by a thousand eyes twice nightly.

The Good Bad Girl is celebrated for her allure but this allure is never allowed to overwhelm the spectator. Besides, she has not got enough self-confidence to overwhelm men. She has to rely on a childlike charm, she has more in common with Mary

Pickford than with Mae West; she must make up to the pae-
dophile in men, in order to reassure both men and herself that
her own sexuality will not reveal to them their own inadequacy.
And, like Justine, she cannot judge; her innocence is prelap-
sarian, she does not know the difference between good and evil,
only that between nice and nasty.

Her innocence, furthermore, forbids her to solicit. Her innocence is her own excuse for her own object status; she cannot
solicit because she does not know how to desire. She is always
the prey, never the hunter, and 'The most innocent are tor-
mented the most,' says the Sadeian libertine in *The Hundred
and Twenty Days at Sodom*. But she does not understand that.

Above all, she discovers she must not take her own allure
seriously. She must laugh it off. The beautiful creature must
become a comedienne. She will adopt the pathetic devices of
the sexless clown as a means of protection from her pursuers.
That a lovely woman is always, in essence, a comic figure, even
in tragic art in the modern period, is curiously exemplified in
Frank Wedekind's 'Lulu' plays, *Earth Spirit* and *Pandora's Box*.
Throughout the action of both plays a conspicuous part of the
decor is the portrait of the beautiful and sexually free Lulu
dressed as Pierrot, the moonstruck clown of *commedia dell' arte*.
This is surely a modern phenomenon, this downgrading of the
physical value of the imperiously attractive woman;
Shakespeare would scarcely have allowed the action of *Antony
and Cleopatra* to be dominated by a portrait of his heroine
dressed in the cap and bells of the court fool. But this one must
make fun of herself because she can never admit she knows *why*
she is pretty. Lulu herself certainly guesses why she is pretty; and
Jack the Ripper must stab her to show her how her prettiness is

itself the source of sin. In an attempt to avoid this unpleasant denouement, the pretty girl must voluntarily remove her boobs and buttocks from the armoury of the seductress. She must pretend she cannot understand how they got there, in the first place.

Soon they lose even the significance of the conventional attributes of the female; they become the signs of a denaturised being, as if there was an inherent freakishness about breasts and buttocks at the best of times, as if half the human race were not equipped with them. As if they were as surprising and unusual physical appurtenances to find on a woman as fins or wings.

The world breathes a sigh of relief; voluntary castration! She has desexed herself by acknowledging how comic her sexuality is; she is prepared to allow her tits and bum to turn into cues for raucous laughter, like a clown's red nose and baggy pants. They become no more than signs that provoke mirth. Groucho twitches his eyebrows and gnaws his moustache when Monroe can't think why she is being followed; he knows the joke is on her. Her ignorance of the erotic disturbance she creates is the product of her comic innocence and so she is denied even the possession of her self, just as that innocence shows how easy she will be to deceive. And she will not answer back; isn't she dumb, after all? She has torn herself off Lulu's crucifix of the tragic heroine to set herself up in the invisible pillory of the stand-up comic.

The milk bottle joke in Frank Tashlin's 'fifties movie, *The Girl Can't Help It*, illustrates perfectly this comic degradation. Jayne Mansfield clutches the milk bottles to her mammaries, a crude reminder as to the primary function of these glands – no, they are not orbs of delight; by no means that magic place where Freud, the romantic, thought that love and hunger met . . . they are farcical globes of fat and their function is more hygienically superseded by any dairy.

The Beautiful Blonde Clowns, Jean Harlow, Judy Holliday, Jayne Mansfield, a sisterhood of unfortunate Js, as if the name Justine lingered on as a race memory in the casting offices, all die young. All are Justine in her final degradation. Now she must endlessly apologise for the insulting lavishness of her physical equipment, which is a ceaseless embarrassment to her. But the laughter she invokes as a protection against the knowledge of her own sexuality is itself a form of the desecration she attempted to protect herself against by laughing at herself first of all.

She hopes to disarm, to endear by her ignorance of her own seductiveness, as Justine did when she went to see the priest in her little white dress and was – 'the men keep following me' – kissed for her trouble. But Sade had a tragic sense of life and did not find anything to laugh at in Justine's humiliation. The Beautiful Clown must endure laughter although she is comic only because she is ignorant of her power to compel, to attract, to receive voluntarily that submission from others which others force on her.

She has fostered her own innocence, her own stupidity, as an insulation from the pain of her endless humiliations; therefore, exiled from her own allure, she does not know how much her allure deviates from the norm and, by doing so, suggests the inadequacy of the whole theory of the norm. She will not be loved, as she hopes to be, because she is so beautiful, such a perturbation, a challenge that continues to exist after it has been met; she will only be resented.

She intends the exhibition of her vulnerability will avert hostility and elicit cherishing. She thinks that if she says: 'See how much you have hurt me!' she will halt the punishment, but the punishment continues. It sharpens, since its object was the infliction of that pain her helpless protest has just confirmed.

She is not in control of the laughter and contempt she arouses. They are in control of her, modifying her opinion of herself, indignifying her.

In herself, this lovely ghost, this zombie, or woman who has never been completely born as a woman, only as a debased cultural idea of a woman, is appreciated only for her decorative value. Final condition of the imaginary prostitute: men would rather have slept with her than sleep with her. She is most arousing as a memory or as a masturbatory fantasy. If she perceives herself as something else, the contradictions of her situation will destroy her. This is the Monroe syndrome.

She has never perceived her appearance as a quality of herself but as something extraneous to her. She is afraid men only want her because she is beautiful so she is denied any use at all of her appearance, which exists for her only as a reflection in the eyes of spectators at a humiliation, at the spectacle of her distress, which gives the witnesses so much pleasure. She might be vain; she cannot be proud. And, because she is beautiful, she arouses concupiscence. Therefore she knows in her heart she must be bad. If she is bad, then it is right she should be punished. She is always ready for more suffering. She is always ready for more suffering because she is always ready to please. 'That's how I like women!' exclaims Saint Fond in *Juliette*, when a girl he is torturing bursts into tears.

Justine is the model for the nineteenth and early twentieth-century denial of femininity as praxis, the denial of femininity as a positive mode of dealing with the world. Worst of all, a cultural conspiracy has deluded Justine and her sisters into a belief that their dear being is in itself sufficient contribution to the world; so they present the enigmatic image of irresistibility and powerlessness, forever trapped in impotence.

III THE TOAD ON THE ROSE

Noirceuil, lover of Justine's sister, describes the perfect object of the lust of the libertine, who acknowledges no law except that of his senses' pleasure:

Beauty, virtue, innocence, candour, misfortune – the object of our lust finds no protection in any of these qualities. On the contrary. Beauty arouses us further; virtue, innocence, candour enhance the object; misfortune puts it into our power, renders it amenable to us; so, all those qualities tend only to excite us still further and we should look on them all as simply fuel for our passions. These qualities also afford us the opportunity of violating another prohibition; I mean offer us the kind of pleasure we get from sacrilege, or the profanation of objects that expect our worship. That beautiful girl is an object of reverence only for fools; when I make her the target of my keenest and coarsest appetites, I experience the double pleasure of sacrificing to my appetites both a beautiful object and one before which the crowd bows down.

Sade's sexual metaphor is always ambiguous. Linguistically, he mystifies the sexual attributes of the female body; it is described in sacred terms, even in terms of sacred architecture, as though it were a holy place. The female orifice is a shrine, a place of worship. The surgeon, Roland, apostrophises the cunt: 'temple of my long-loved pleasures'. This ironic sacralisation of the female body is used throughout Sade; even in its mortification, when it is spattered with blood and ordure, the altar retains its perfidious magic. Incense is burned at this altar; ejaculation is regularly 'the burning of incense', at the altars Nature intends for such homage. Orgasm itself is often described as the rendering of homage. This homage is itself equivocal, administered with such violence the recipient may regard it as sacrilege, the culmination of an act of pure hostility.

Now and then, Sade kitschifies the prick itself, calling it 'the first agent of love's pleasure', but, more often, it is a mechanical device, an engine or an instrument of warfare, a weapon. And, frequently, it is a snake. 'The snake emits its venom'; 'the serpent is about to discharge its venom.' When Justine sees Jerome, the licentious monk, insert his prick into the mouth of a young girl prisoner in the monastery of St Mary-in-the-Wood, she thinks of: 'the filthy reptile withering the rose'. Sexual approach is as much a defilement as a tribute, yet the very act of defilement reinforces the holiness of the temple. In a secular world, the notion of the impure is meaningless. Only a true believer can see the pure glamour of the blasphemy. In Sade's lengthiest piece of proscriptive Utopian writing: *Yet Another Effort, Frenchmen, If You Would Become Republicans*, the female sexual organs are referred to as 'common fountains'. It is impossible for such things to be defiled. But the egalitarian utopia of the republic is, as yet, unachieved; we must still deal with notions of dirt and transgression.

So it is necessary for the young girl, the virgin, the rose, the *rosa mundi* or Blessed Virgin, to be of exceptional beauty. Her beauty in itself excites abuse because it has helped to make her an object of reverence. Her expectation of reverence ensures her passivity and her weakness and also her horrid surprise when the state of grace in which she believes she exists is abruptly revoked.

Justine begins her miserable career with the idea she never quite rids herself of, that her beauty and virtue are in themselves qualities which demand respect. Beauty, youth and innocence in women give them an artificial ascendancy over a world that allots them love and admiration to precisely the extent a beautiful, young and innocent woman is deprived of the ability to act in the world. She is compensated for her defencelessness by a convention of respect which is largely false. Herself mystified by herself, narcissistically enamoured of the idea of herself as Blessed Virgin, she has no notion at all of who she is except in fantasy. To the extent that she has been made holy and thinks of herself as such, so she is capable of being desecrated. Purity is always in danger.

The girls imprisoned for the pleasure of the monks in the monastery of St Mary-in-the-Wood are all from well-to-do, 'distinguished' families. 'There is not one who cannot claim the highest rank, not one who is not treated with the greatest disrespect.' The libertines in *The Hundred and Twenty Days at Sodom* belong to a supper club when they are at home in Paris. There they hold four parties a week, one of which is especially reserved for the abuse and humiliation of girls of the upper classes. In addition they hold a regular weekly supper attended by four young women of the aristocracy who have been kidnapped from their parents' homes and are now prostituted. These girls are particularly vilely treated. When the libertines plan their holiday at the Chateau of Silling, they stipulate that the procuresses should find them victims from the most eminent families; for these services, the agents are paid thirty thousand francs a victim.

It is upon the women of the upper classes, whose beauty and chastity is a function of class and whom universal admiration has always acquitted of the need to be human, that the licentious wrath of the libertines falls most heavily. These girls are chastised because they expect to be admired and are raped because they have put too high a value on their own sexuality. Their sexual abstinence is a form, almost, of conspicuous consumption; it is an ostentatious luxury that is not available to women from a class that can achieve financial independence only through the practice of some form of prostitution. They overvalue their chastity in the way that certain modern women overvalue their orgasmic potential: both overvaluations are aspects of elitism.

However, the submissiveness the young ladies learned at their expensive boarding schools stands the libertines in good stead. The girls will not fight back. They do not know that it is possible for them to do so. The frigidity they had been taught to equate with virtue prevents them from achieving a sexual autonomy that would transform their passive humiliations into a form of action. Not only can they never feel pleasure in the embraces of their violators nor even admit it might be possible to do so, but, poor girls, they will always feel horror, revulsion and fear because they believe indifference to lust is as immoral as lust itself.

The princess of the fairy tale is reduced to the condition of the whore in the gutter; the fury of the libertines works this reversal. But, since the princess still retains her consciousness of herself as princess rather than acquiring the self-possession of a whore, she has been truly degraded.

The libertines show her that the qualities that made her precious can easily be stripped from her. They thrust her face-down on the bed and turn their attentions to her arse, that part of herself reverence has always particularly denied existed. They force her to publicly perform excretory activity she has always conducted furtively, in private, as if it were an activity that in itself degraded her, an activity too human, too common to be publicly acknowledged by such a rare creature as herself. (Swift exclaimed in horror: 'Celia shits!' How can it be possible such a precious being, all angel and no ape, should ever do such a thing? God must be very cruel, to shatter our illusions so.)

Her final humiliation is to realise that her value has never resided in herself but in the values of the open market; now the princess has a price tag thrust upon her. Like a common criminal, she has a price on her head. As if she were a cake, she is bought and sold.

Hitherto, like a porcelain figure, she had presented a glazed surface to the world. Her surfaces seemed too smooth, too impermeable to be fissured by any kind of feeling. But now, under the lash, splashed with excrement, deluged in spunk, she exhibits unmistakable evidence of common humanity. She screams, she pleads, she weeps. Pain, in triumph, has found a foothold on a carapace that had seemed too smooth to hold it.

When she suffers, she exists. She will embrace her newly discovered masochism with all her heart because she has found a
sense of being through suffering.

IV MORAL OF JUSTINE

Belmore, the immolator of small boys, suggests to his good
friend, Juliette, Justine's sister, in the sequel *to Justine* that the
origin of the unnatural reverence for women which finds its
expression in the forms of romantic love derives from the professions of witchcraft and prophecy that women exercised in
the antique past. To a man freed from ignorant superstition, says
Belmore, women are no more than sexual receptacles, pieces of
plumbing. All mystification stripped from her, Celia does not
only shit; she becomes herself a commode.

Wives and mothers are sanctified by usage and convention;
on them falls the greatest wrath. In the monastery of St Mary-
in-the-Wood, pregnancy means a death sentence. Juliette
tortures pregnant women during her holiday in Florence. The
worst tortures of the Castle of Silling in *The Hundred and
Twenty Days at Sodom* are reserved for the pregnant Constance.
Madame de Mistival, wife and mother, the object of the fury of
her daughter in *Philosophy in the Boudoir*, is utterly desanctified.
Her motherliness is stripped from her in a ferocious rite of exor-
cism; her own daughter rapes her. In Sade's brothels, husbands
prostitute wives; husbands force their wives to witness the prostitution of daughters.

The mother herself is taken from her shrine, the holy
family, and turned over to the world, the public brothel,

communalised, secularised, restored to a state of natural or original impurity from which her wifehood and mothering was a falling away. Clairwil, Juliette's accomplice, says: 'Libertinage in women used once to be venerated the world over; it had worshippers everywhere, even temples.' Not fucking but continence is the offence against nature. But the mother in her holiness does not understand that. She will accept punishment because it enhances her status in her own eyes but she will never tolerate the notion of pleasure, since pleasure robs procreation of its aspect of duty.

The ironic worshippers approach the temple and raze it to the ground. The libertines turn the Blessed Virgin over on her belly and sodomise her, transforming the hole nature intended for simple evacuation into an aperture for complex pleasure. Holy Mother says sex is sanctified only in the service of reproduction; nonsense! cry the libertines. The inversion of regular practice transforms the significance of the practice. A simple inversion then becomes a complex transformation. 'Love has pitched his palace in the place of excrement,' said Crazy Jane to the Bishop. The backside, the anus, the areas of the body the consecration of Beauty denies become desirable.

Once desired, they, too, become beautiful.

The libertines in *The Hundred and Twenty Days at Sodom* take four hideous and aged crones with them on their holiday at the castle. The sexual enthusiasm they exhibit for the wrinkled and ulcerated old monsters is an ironic reversal of the veneration of physical beauty; human ugliness at its most extreme is as extraordinary a phenomenon as beauty and a phenomenon of the same kind, one of excess. So why may it not, too, be appetising? And, like the beautiful girls and boys, the monstrous old women are tortured and killed; they must pay the high price of their own desirability as soon as they are desired.

To be the *object* of desire is to be defined in the passive case.

To exist in the passive case is to die in the passive case – that is, to be killed.

This is the moral of the fairy tale about the perfect woman.

Paradoxically, Justine's only triumph is her refusal to treat herself as a thing, although everybody she meets does. Since this awareness of herself is not shared by anybody else, it remains a victory in a void. She is the bourgeois individualist in its tragic aspect; her sister, Juliette, offers its heroic side. Both are women whose identities have been defined exclusively by men.

THREE

Sexuality as Terrorism: The Life of Juliette

Time is a man, space is a woman, and her masculine portion is death.

Vision of the Last Judgement, William Blake

I MAKING IT

The life of Juliette exists in a dialectical relationship to that of her sister. The vision of the inevitable prosperity of vice, as shown in her triumphant career, and the vision of the inevitable misfortunes of virtue that Justine's life offers do not cancel one another out; rather, they mutually reflect and complement one another, like a pair of mirrors. Each story has the same moral, offered at many levels, which may be summed up as: the comfort of one class depends on the misery of another class. There is no room in Sade's impeccable logic for the well-upholstered wishful thinking that would like the poor to have more money if that did not mean we ourselves had less. To be a woman is to be automatically at a disadvantage in a man's world, just like being poor, but to be a woman is a more easily remedied condition. If she abandons the praxis of femininity, then it is easy enough to enter the class of the rich, the men, provided one enters it on the terms of that class.

The life of Juliette proposes a method of profane mastery of the instruments of power. She is a woman who acts according to the precepts and also the practice of a man's world and so she does not suffer. Instead, she causes suffering.

'It was no accident that the Marquis de Sade chose heroines and not heroes,' said Guillaume Apollinaire. 'Justine is woman as she has been until now, enslaved, miserable and less than human; her opposite, Juliette, represents the woman whose advent he anticipated, a figure of whom minds have as yet no conception, who is rising out of mankind, who will have wings and who will renew the world.' Seventy years ago, Apollinaire could equate Juliette with the New Woman; it is not so easy to do so today, although Juliette remains a model for women, in some ways. She is rationality personified and leaves no single cell of her brain unused. She will never obey the fallacious promptings of her heart. Her mind functions like a computer programmed to produce two results for herself – financial profit and libidinal gratification. By the use of her reason, an intellectual apparatus women themselves are still inclined to undervalue, she rids herself of some of the more crippling aspects of femininity; but she is a New Woman in the mode of irony.

She is, just as her sister is, a description of a type of female behaviour rather than a model of female behaviour and her triumph is just as ambivalent as is Justine's disaster. Justine is the thesis, Juliette the antithesis; both are without hope and neither pays any heed to a future in which might lie the possibility of a synthesis of their modes of being, neither submissive nor aggressive, capable of both thought and feeling.

If Justine is a pawn because she is a woman, Juliette transforms herself from pawn to queen in a single move and henceforward goes wherever she pleases on the chess board. Nevertheless, there remains the question of the presence of the king, who remains the lord of the game.

Like *The Misfortunes of Virtue*, *The Prosperities of Vice* is also a black fairy tale; but it is Justine-through-the-looking glass, an inversion of an inversion, so that it has a happy ending in which true lovers are united and good fortune smiles on everyone. The immense, picaresque narrative relates with precision every detail of Juliette's career. Juliette performs all the crimes of which Justine is falsely accused, and is never punished for them; instead she is rewarded because she does not submit to the law at all. She does not need to submit to the law; she is in complicity with the law and it is adjusted, if not made, for her benefit. She sleeps with the makers of the laws and caters to their picturesque sexual needs; she knows their weak spots, and indulges them, and so she has their Mafia-like protection. Further, the pain inflicted on Justine is transformed into Juliette's pleasure, by the force of Juliette's will and desire for self-mastery and heightened extremes of experience. Juliette has learned to take pleasure from pain and herself demands that delicious excitation of the nerves; and nothing will scar the thick skin of this well-fleshed brunette, who knows how to do her own soliciting and is never the sexual prey, except for the sake of a ruse or a game.

Juliette's life is like the reign of Tamburlaine the Great, an arithmetical progression of atrocities. If we admire the campaigns of a great general, is it hypocrisy to refuse to admire Juliette's? If her life is also, as is Justine's life, a pilgrimage towards death – for even Juliette must die – in a world governed by god, the king and the law, the trifold masculine symbolism of authority, then Juliette knows better than her sister how useless it is to rebel against fate. She is so much in control of herself she may not even do this unconsciously.

The story of Juliette begins, not where the version of *Justine* of 1791 ends, with a repentant Juliette entering a convent, but at the beginning of Juliette's own autobiography after a rather more extravagant version of the life of Justine herself. We return to Juliette's boudoir and Justine herself is there to listen to Juliette's story. The novel will end with another, profane, version of the death of Justine.

Juliette's story-telling function is itself part of her whoreishness. She is a perfect whore, like the whores in *The Hundred and Twenty Days at Sodom*. In that book, four libertines take four of the most brilliant and distinguished prostitutes in Paris off for a holiday to the remote and isolated Castle of Silling, besides a numerous complement of wives, servants and victims. These four women survive the ensuing holocaust; they will all return home safe and sound, not only because they are consummately wicked, but because, like Scheherazade, they know how to utilise the power of the word, of narrative, to save their lives. The continuity of their narratives protects them from the discontinuity of death. These women, like Juliette, tell the stories of their lives. Their sexual anecdotes determine the form of the orgies in the castle and so they can ensure they themselves will not be sacrificed during any of them. Juliette, the personification of the whore as story-teller, often breaks off her narrative for sexual encounters with her listeners, who are all old friends and occasionally appear as actual actors in it. She leaves a pornographic hole in the text on purpose for them.

For Justine, an unwilling listener, her sister's autobiography and her own involuntary participation in the rituals accompanying it, are another form of martyrdom, the martyrdom of unwilling exposure to pornography.

Juliette's education begins in the convent where she and her sister spent their childhoods. If Justine learned piety and submission there, Juliette learned pleasure and reason. The abbess, Delbène, has been sent to the convent against her will, to spare her parents the expense of a dowry, and she spends her ample leisure inculcating in those young girls in her charge in whom she spies a natural propensity for vice the elements of sexual expertise, the relativity of ethics, militant feminism and doctrinaire atheism. The notion of a natural propensity for vice is essential to Sadeian psychology; vice is innate, as is virtue, if social conditions are unalterable. This straitjacket psychology relates his fiction directly to the black and white ethical world of fairy tale and fable; it is in conflict with his frequently expounded general theory of moral relativity, that good and evil are not the same thing at all times and in all places. So his characters represent moral absolutes in a world where no moral absolutes exist. This is the major contradiction inherent in his fiction, which he never resolves.

Like all Sade's rational women, Delbène prefers her own sex. Juliette is an eager pupil; she gains information, not only from

Delbène, but from a friend who runs away to work in a brothel. Juliette makes friends easily, unlike her sister; solitude is not her quality, even when she is alone, and she is as incapable of introspection as she is incapable of melancholy. Not only has she no inner life; she would deny the existence of such a thing.

For Juliette, the convent is a school of love. Her initiation is completed by a murder, for the convent is also a Sadeian place of privilege where everything is permissible. The Abbess Delbène adopts a mothering relation to Juliette. She is the first and welcomed fairy godmother in Juliette's history, the type of the mature libertine woman who has sharpened her reason and her sex into a weapon. She is an aristocratic and cultured version of the brigand, La Dubois, whose protection Justine refused in the early days of her career. Unlike La Dubois, Delbène has had the means and the opportunity to cultivate her intellect; she reads Spinoza and lectures Juliette on the nature of justice and on the sexual autonomy of women. She has a cold heart, and she murders for pleasure.

The voice of reason, always subversive, must issue from a monster; Sade must censor Delbène, as he creates her. She is rational, therefore wicked.

In Delbène's arms, Juliette nourishes her own special qualities of transgression and sacrilege. From Delbène, she learns a stoicism that serves her well when Delbène turns her out of the convent the moment Juliette's father loses all his money. Delbène is not interested in poor girls. Juliette parts company with the grief-stricken Justine when she sees Justine will not accompany her to the brothel where her friend preceded her. But Juliette herself is eager to learn a trade with which to support herself.

This brothel is an earthly paradise where all the pleasures of the flesh are available, but nothing is free. It is a Sadeian place of privilege; like all brothels in Sade, it is an evil Eden that might, at any moment, turn into hell. It operates with the wholehearted support and approval of the police. In an absolute privacy purchased for cash, all sexual tastes are permissible but it is as if a *cordon sanitaire* surrounds these places. The Sadeian paradise is a model of the world, in its cash-sale structure; and also it is a place of exile from the world, a place of imaginary liberty where the ritual perversions of the libertines contain no element of a taboo freely broken but come to dominate their lives, like the rigid rituals of the Catholic church. Privilege has a negative aspect. It is like the freedom of the outlaw, which only exists in relation to the law itself. Privilege is in itself a denial of common experiences. The brothel presents a closed system, encapsulated from the reality it both mimics and denies. Women rule in the brothel, as in the nursery, which it somewhat resembles; but the economic power lies in the hands of the customers, who can always take their cash elsewhere, or even refuse to pay. So the whores resort to theft.

Theft represents the morality of the outlaw. Duval, the master thief, lectures the girls: 'If you trace the right of property back to its source, you always arrive at usurpation.' Theft, therefore, is a moral imperative; it is a means of redistributing property. Theft, deceit and cunning are the revenges of the weak upon the strong, of the poor upon the rich. One of Juliette's colleagues encourages her to steal for the sake of the principle of human equality; where equality has not been established by chance or fate, it is up to the poor to ensure it by their ingenuity.

The brothel is also a place of lies, of false appearances. Juliette's virginity is sold successively to fifty buyers and, for each customer, she must act out a part – that she is starving and forced to sell herself; that it was her mother who sold her to the brothel. And so on, a series of flattering charades designed to persuade the customers they are not dealing with simple business-women, that the weeping creatures who reluctantly bend themselves to their superior will are, in fact, so many innocent Justines.

Juliette concludes her apprenticeship of flesh by selling her anus to an archbishop. She has already a well-developed taste for anal intercourse; she is proud of her superb arse and the outrageous, unnatural uses to which she puts it. Not only is it a crime, according to the morality of her century, it is also an excellent contraceptive measure, and motherhood, as yet, has no part in her plans.

Now, the last of her virginities gone, she is fully equipped to enter upon a wider stage than that of her first brothel, Madame Duvergier's establishment.

She meets a man of power, the statesman, Noirceuil, who teaches her how Nature made the weak to be the slaves of the strong. She learns her lesson at once; to escape slavery, she must embrace tyranny. All living creatures are born and die in isolation, says Noirceuil; in the cultivation and practice of egoism and self-interest alone may be found true happiness. Juliette is immediately drawn to this credo of bourgeois individualism.

When Noirceuil tells Juliette that he murdered her father, she declares that she loves him and is soon installed in his house as his mistress, with special instructions to torment his wife, whom he designates as a 'mere pleasure machine'. Noirceuil has also instructed her in the rare pleasures of avarice. She returns to Duvergier's brothel, to earn more money in her spare time, for the richer she becomes, the more money she must have.

Duvergier, the madame, is another fairy godmother, although she is not a diabolic one. The most wicked act that she performs is an attempt to foist a syphilitic upon Juliette and she apologises when Juliette angrily rejects him, and goes off to find a substitute harlot, because the syphilitic pays well so she cannot turn him away. If Juliette did indeed accept Duvergier's proffered mother, she might have led the quiet and unexemplary life of a fairly honest whore, in time the mistress of her own establishment. But Juliette has ambitions far beyond this.

The brothel is a place of appearances and lies; it is also a place where paradoxical truths are put into the mouths of those we expect to lie, so you may accept them or not, as you please. If the whores and the thieves have advanced a libertarian – communist theory of the ownership of property, then Duvergier offers a rational distinction between love and fancy. Love, she says, need not cohabit with fidelity; she shows Juliette a room filled with respectably married women all waiting for illicit lovers. Yet not one of these women does not adore nor is not adored by the man with whom she lives. And there is nothing odd about that opines Duvergier cosily! Love is a moral and intellectual passion based on respect and comradeship; the fancies of the flesh are of a different order of experience, not to be despised because they give us so much pleasure but in no way trespassing on the integrity of the heart's affections.

Juliette rewards Duvergier for her good advice and cherishing by, later, poisoning her.

Juliette is well-paid by Noirceuil. She steals. She sells herself on the side. She prospers, until she falls foul of a certain Duke whom she has robbed and he has her thrown in prison. Noirceuil rescues her on condition she incriminates an innocent girl for the crime; the unfortunate are the playthings of the rich.

By this act of false witness, Juliette puts herself firmly in the camp of the masters. Like her sister, she feels no natural bond between herself and other women; why should she? Her circumstances are not those of most women. She has no sense of women as a class; it is difficult to ascertain whether Sade does so himself. Sade regularly subsumes women to the general class of the weak and therefore the exploited, and so he sees femininity as a mode of experience that transcends gender. Feminine impotence is a quality of the poor, regardless of sex. Juliette is an exception; by the force of her will, she will become a Nietzschean superwoman, which is to say, a woman who has transcended her gender but not the contradictions inherent in it.

After this brush with justice, Juliette is ready to be introduced to the representatives of the law. Noirceuil invites her to a dinner party to meet Saint Fond, one of whose activities is the distribution of warrants for arbitrary arrest. Another guest is D'Albert, chief justice of the Parlement de Paris, who promises Juliette a life-long immunity from punishment under the law. Saint Fond makes Juliette lick his arse, after dinner: 'Kneel and face it; consider the honour I do you in permitting you to do my arse the homage an entire nation, no, the whole world aspires to give it!' Sade occasionally, if confusingly, some-times says exactly what he means. The interminable arse-licking his characters engage in is nothing more than metaphor made concrete.

Coprophagy is one of the rarest sexual variations but it plays a large part in Sade's lexicon of sexual activity. Juliette soon accustoms herself to eating the shit of the great. In *The Hundred and Twenty Days at Sodom*, the four libertines who rule the castle always take a victim or two with them to the privy, to clean their arses for them. This is the way to court the favour of the great, to gently cleanse their maculated assholes with a cunning tongue. If you do it long enough, it becomes second nature; you hardly notice the taste. Not the pursuit of erotic pleasure but enlightened self-interest has overcome the barrier of disgust.

For the libertines themselves, it is a different matter. They, too, gladly eat shit but they control its production. An elabor-ate bureaucracy is established to govern the production and distribution of faecal matter in *The Hundred and Twenty Days at Sodom*. The victims are placed on special diets, to ensure the quality and flavour of the turds. Saint Fond will put Juliette on a similar diet, for the same reason, and instruct her how to take care of her health to safeguard his own. The libertines become veritable connoisseurs of the turd, comparing vintages and bou-quets with the mincing pedantry of the wine snob.

But the excremental activity of the victims who produce these comestibles is governed by rigid sanctions. In the Castle of Silling, the victims may shit only at certain times of the day and then only with permission of the masters, who may refuse at whim. The involuntary production of shit is severely punished.

The nature of production-consumption relation of shit in Sade is illuminated by a psychoanalytic interpretation. The faeces are the child's first gift. He can give them or withhold them at whim; utilising his excremental production, he can cause his mother delight or distress since, by producing them, he expresses active compliance with his environment and, by retaining them, disaffection. With his shit, he expresses obedience or disobedience. Before he can speak, his excretions are the child's means of expression – shit and tears; in this, he is just like the victims in the castle. He is, however, more in control of his shit than he is of his weepings. Excretion is his first concrete production and, through it, the child gains his first experience of labour relations. He may reserve the right to go on excremental strike or to engage in a form of faecal offensive. The excremental faculty is a manipulative device and to be baulked of the free control of it is to be deprived of the first, most elementary, expression of autonomy. The victims of the libertines may not shit when and as they please; they are under the severest restraints in this particular. But the masters are perfectly free to roll at will in their own ordure, to.be as clean or as filthy as they please, to exercise total excremental liberty. This is a sign of their mastery, to return, as adults, freely, to a condition of infantilism.

The libertines acknowledge the turd as gift. 'Let me eat her gift,' says a coprophagic customer of the prostitute-narrator, Duclos, in *The Hundred and Twenty Days at Sodom*. But these gifts are always extorted. The gifts are brutally ravished from the owners, produced on order according to contract in the brothel and by Juliette, or in fear of force in the castle. The libertines usurp the primary physical freedom of the body. They monopolise the elementary productions of the bodies of others and arbitrarily regulate involuntary physical functions.

The coprophagic passions of the libertines reflect their exhaustive greed. The anal Juliette has an appropriately anal passion for capital accumulation. There is more to coprophagy than a particularly exotic perversion that requires an extraordinary degree of mastery of disgust to be able to indulge in it; the coprophage's taste asserts the function of flesh as a pure means of production in itself. His economic sense, alert even in the grip of passion, insists that even the waste products of the flesh must not be wasted. All must be consumed.

The coprophiliac Saint Fond, who demands that even his own waste products should be treated with reverence, employs Juliette as his procuress and his poisoner at a fabulous salary. Her first task in this position is to poison Noirceuil's wife; her next, to poison Saint Fond's father. Her relation with Noirceuil contains a great deal of the affection characteristic of Sadeian comrades in crime; that with Saint Fond is based more on self-interest tinged with fear. But now she makes her first truly significant relationship; she becomes the friend of the beautiful and terrible Madame de Clairwil, who prides herself upon never having shed a tear.

Her relation with Clairwil is, at first, not quite one of equals although Juliette never adopts a subservient role to her. Juliette is more beautiful than she; she does not frighten men so much and this gives her a tactical advantage over her friend but there is no element of rivalry between them, for Clairwil is a great aristocrat, born to power of her own. She does not need men to validate her power, as Juliette does. But she is less resilient than Juliette because she is less flexible. Juliette, child of a banker and hence a daughter of the bourgeoisie, is the representative of a rising class, the class that will dominate the coming century, and Clairwil's aristocratic ascendancy is on the wane. The ease with which Juliette robs princes and, later, with which she disposes of the Princess Borghese when she gets tired of her, also suggests the aristocracy no longer have the power that the politicians, Noirceuil and Saint Fond wield.

Nevertheless, she and Clairwil have enough in common to feel themselves sisters. Later, they will pose as sisters. Both belong to the same maenad and violent sisterhood of female libertines and so form a terrible alliance, like avenging angels who are always in complicity with the seat of power; they remain angels of the lord. Having acceded, as women, to the world of men, their mastery of that world reveals its mono-maniac inhumanity to the full, just as Justine's incompetence trapped in the circumstances of her life as a woman, also did. Their liberation from the limitations of femininity is a personal one, for themselves only. They gratify themselves fully but it is a liberation without enlightenment and so becomes an instrument for the oppression of others, both women and men. One of Sade's cruellest lessons is that tyranny is implicit in all privilege. My freedom makes you more unfree, if it does not acknowledge your freedom, also.

Clairwil's monstrous lusts encompass murder and she hates men far more than Juliette does. It is men she loves to murder: 'I adore avenging my sex for the horrors men subject us to when the monsters have the upper hand.' Her beauty is the cruel beauty of the Medusa; she overwhelms and dominates whereas Juliette, more cunning, is content to seduce. Clairwil's rationality is allied with wit and her atheism has a kind of wild glory about it. Her castratory rage is intellectually qualified; she has always felt herself debased by the mere sight of men. Only men arouse her to serious cruelties. She is an 'enragée', like some of the furious women of the French Revolution, but her rage extends only to her own nymphomaniac passions, that reduce the men upon whom she inflicts her vengeance to disembodied phalli. She has no other use for them. She is dedicated to sexual warfare and will, as the sequel to an orgy in a Carmelite monastery during which she and Juliette have exhausted every single one of the inmates, shear off the handsome prick of a young friar, embalm it and use it for a dildo.

Clairwil's enthusiasm for the depersonalised prick, the sublime penis, is boundless. After she dies, she claims, a dissection will find a penis growing in her brain; her desire is so great that she has incorporated the desired object in herself, but, unassimilated, it still retains its own form. This is one of the contradictions of Sade's female libertines, that they ingest but do not integrate within themselves the signs of maleness.

Juliette is now obscenely rich and lives with obscene opulence. During a famine, she finds herself unable to give charity to the starving because of the expenses she has incurred in a project for building mirrored boudoirs in her park, in the purchase of statues for her garden, in improving her lawns. It gives her great pleasure to deny charity; if it gives her so much pleasure *not* to do good, she reasons, must it not give her still greater pleasure to do evil? As soon as the decision is made, she moves firmly from the passive to the active, to gratuitous crime, and Clairwil puts her up for membership of a unique club, the Sodality of the Friends of Crime.

The Sodality is an institution of the highest privilege. It is a model of a society entirely devoted to libidinous gratification, like the Castle of Silling in *The Hundred and Twenty Days at Sodom* and the monastery of St Mary-in-the-Wood and so it is like a nursery as it might be if the children themselves had the sole running of it, and it is also like a concentration camp from the point of view of the guards. It is itself a secularised monastery; indeed, it is a post-humanist, ironic version of Rabelais's Abbey of Thélème, which had as its only rule the exhortation: 'Do what thou wilt.' This is certainly the motto of the Sodality. But Rabelais believed no rules were required 'because men that are free, well-born, well-bred and conversant in honest companies, have naturally an instinct and spurre that prompteth them unto vertuous actions, and withdraws them from vice.' No such considerations apply here. Like all Utopias, its literary and political origin is the Republic of Plato, which the Sodality curiously resembles in its inflexibility and elitism; a parodic Good Society, supported by wealth, power and immunity from the law.

The luxuriously appointed premises of the Sodality are fitted up with seraglios, printshops and torture chambers; it runs its own kitchens and its own cab-ranks, self-feeding and self-transporting. It is a society in miniature in which nobody engages in productive labour nor wears any clothes except the ritual uniform of nakedness which is a mark of the members' elite status. Even their skins have become signs of rank. Here, the price of pleasure is death but not the death of any of the initiates. The Sodality is divided into three classes: the libertines; their victims; and their servants, the cooks, harem keepers, torturers and nurses who are immune from harm because they are useful. Their serviceability precludes their victimisation. Unlike Plato, however, Sade allows a token handful of artists to enter this sacrosanct domain, at a cheap rate. This is like a little pre-figuration of Marcuse's theory of repressive sublimation; if artists are allowed a taste of some of the wild joys of privilege, they will throw their lots in with the masters immediately. If art is indeed, as Sade defined it, 'the perpetual immoral subversion of the existing order', the artist is emasculated the moment he enters, with the complimentary ticket he has accepted with such humiliating eagerness and gratitude, the brothels of the ruling class. This might also apply to Juliette herself.

The Sodality is dedicated to atheism and its members acknowledge none of the familial and marital bonds that they have outside its doors. All dissolve on entering the Sodality's premises. Its privilege extends to all areas of sexual taboo. Expulsion is guaranteed for good works. The president and all the officers are elected by secret ballot; in a community of equals, the libertines observe egalitarian relations with one another. Any woman or any man may be elected president, even if the rules for women members of the Sodality state cat-egorically that women 'are created for the pleasure of man'. The egalitarianism of the Sodality extends only to the mem-bers of the class of masters, however. The Sodality, with its rules, its system, its free ballots, its torture chambers, its acknowledgement of the diabolism of privacy, its mutual regard among its members, is the most systematic and depraved of Sade's inverted Edens. Even the Castle of Silling allows more humanity to its victims.

Juliette is now visited by her father, who, it turns out, never died at all, although her mother did; he was ruined and forced into hiding. He reappears with all the unexpectedness of picaresque fiction, a good and virtuous man moved to tears to meet his daughter again. She easily seduces him, is impregnated by him, murders him and subsequently aborts his child; so she rids herself of the spectre of his paternal authority over her by a systematic series of ritual transgressions. She absorbs his essence and then excretes it. Justine weeps to hear all this. Juliette's patricidal embrace and the infanticide which is the completion of the banishment of the father from her life seems the completion of some form of apprenticeship; she is now ready to enter the ranks of the sexual instructresses and Noirceuil entrusts her with the education of his new wife, Saint Fond's daughter. But the girl does not show herself an apt pupil. She will not join Juliette and Clairwil in the camaraderie of libertine superwomen. Instead, she will be sexually martyrised for her husband's pleasure, just as all his other wives have been.

Now Juliette is ready to meet the poisoner, Durand, who has used the formal methods of reason to become a witch. Durand's primal powers are precisely those of enlightenment and reason, put at the service of nihilism. She quotes Archimedes; 'give me a lever big enough and I will move the world', but, for herself, it is a herb that might poison the world she wants. She is a biochemist and her area of study is natural poison. Her profession is the sale of death.

Durand has mastered this world so well that she can foretell the future and she forecasts the death of Clairwil. She is the greatest, most monstrous, most potent of all Sade's cruel godmothers. Her habits are those of the wicked stepmother of fairy tale, the ogre queens who devour babies, and her sexual ambivalence is hermaphroditic. Though she is well past the age of child-bearing, she is extraordinarily beautiful and she is prepared to adopt Juliette as her daughter. The crimes and libertinage of Durand will become the protection and the pleasures of her beloved. But not yet; having introduced herself to the two women, she vanishes, with the suddenness of magic.

Saint Fond now takes Juliette into his complete confidence, and outlines a scheme for the devastation of France which will result in immense profits for himself. He will raze the schools and poorhouses to the ground; send the country to war, the most profitable of all speculations; and produce a famine by his monopoly of the supply of corn. He suggests that Juliette assist him. When she hears his proposals, she shudders and, for this involuntary show of horror, she is doomed. Saint Fond sees her shudder and decides to kill her. Her friend, Noirceuil, warns her; she runs away at once, abandoning her mansions, her safes filled with money, her bank accounts. Her flights, her peregrinations are as involuntary as her sister's but her life does not have the form of a pilgrimage, more of a battle campaign, and now she beats a strategic retreat. However much money she leaves behind, ever forethoughtful, she always manages to conceal a little around her person, that person which is in itself her capital.

She opens a gambling house at Angers and prospers. Soon, she marries the virtuous Count de Lorsanges, cuckolds him, bears him a daughter, poisons him, inherits all and, rich once again, abandons her child to travel to Italy, posing as a rich courtesan. Now she aspires to the highest style. Her friends and clients are kings and princes, all persons of unspeakable wickedness. Her whoreishness is her preservation since she acts as a kind of Figaro of vice, the servant who maintains the instruments of control whilst adopting the attitudes of submission. Control, method, system are Juliette's qualities.

Yet Juliette has a passion for volcanoes, which seem to her the image of the strength and indifference of nature. Whilst gazing into the crater of a volcano, she and her companions – for, unlike Justine, she is never without a faithful entourage – are captured by the cannibal giant, Minski, who lives in a castle in the middle of a lake, a place of privilege with a strong symbolic resemblance to the great original of all places of privilege, the womb. Minski's castle is furnished with girls – chairs, tables, sideboards all formed of the living flesh of captive women. He has reduced women to their final use function, 'thingified' them into sofas, tables and candelabras. His wealth is a guarantee he will live on in this fashion undisturbed. Juliette drugs him and escapes with her friends and his treasure, assuring the castle full of victims they have released from their dungeons that Minski is dead. The victims rejoice; when he wakes up from his drugged sleep, he will kill them all. How Juliette and her maids laugh to think of this denouement.

Now she travels to Florence, opens a brothel, grows infinitely rich, robs her customers as if theft were a form of sexuality or sexuality of theft, commits many murders and moves on to Rome, the holy city.

Rome is significant for Juliette for two reasons. First, she makes another bosom friend, the wicked and beautiful Princess Olympe de Borghese. If Clairwil, the man-hater who has absorbed the phallus, the sign of maleness, into her own brain, is savagery and lucidity, then the velvet, indolent Borghese is a pure voluptuary; her crimes are part of her vicious sensuality and are not the fruit of a steely process of self-discipline. She is a princess and wickedness is as natural to her as breathing. She is a glutton for pleasure, like a huge, cruel cat and cruel as a cat is sleepily cruel, by nature. She lives for sensual excess and pain is a judicious sharpening of her senses. Her tastes tend towards the rococo, the decorative; her orgies require the presence of menageries of animals and the deformed, dwarves, geriatrics, hermaphrodites.

She loves to keep captives and would like to enslave entire nations but, also, she would like to be a public whore, the butt, the plaything, the victim of libertines, desiring at the same time to enslave and be herself enslaved. A certain hysteria characterises her. Like the Italy in which she lives, she is so ripe that she is rotten.

Juliette's second acquaintance in Rome is the Pope himself. This Pope, like many of his predecessors, is a profligate atheist. His coprophilia is a statement of his apostasy: 'I worship shit.' Juliette participates in an orgy at the altar of St Peter's, a venue of, simultaneously, privilege and sacrilege. There are further murderous orgies in the Sistine Chapel; these are the most fitting shrines for crime, opines Sade. After robbing the Pope of a vast sum of money, Juliette sets out for fresh infamies in Naples. Once more, she is captured on the way; again, her capture is a fortunate one. The brigand chief, Brisatesta, takes her to his moated castle at the peak of a mountain but his wife, the sister with whom he lives, gives a cry of joy when she sees Juliette; there will be no tortures for this captive, for Brisatesta's incestuous wife is none other than Clairwil. The two women fall into one another's arms. By a happy accident, the next wayfarer brought captive to the castle proves to be

Juliette's new friend, Borghese, and she, too, is reprieved and feasted.

Brisatesta now tells his life story. This is interesting because of its account of a comprehensive Sadeian education. He and Clairwil were grounded thoroughly in libertinage at the hands of their father and his mistress, their governess. Their mother took part in the anatomy lessons only under duress; at one point, Brisatesta bit off her nipple and, finally, at his father's request, murdered her. Next, inspired by greed for his inheritance, he murdered his father and set out on his travels – Europe, the Netherlands, Sweden and at last Russia, growing richer and more wicked with every crime along the way. In Russia, he met Catherine the Great, a Sadeian malefic despot, the Messalina of all the Russias, and became her lover but, when he bungled the poisoning of the Tsarevitch, she sent Brisatesta to Siberia. He escaped to Turkey and an eventual reunion with his beloved sister; she has abandoned Paris for him and they now devote themselves to domesticity, brigandage and orgiastic recreations in their mountain fastness. A marriage of true minds, they are a model Sadeian couple.

But Clairwil's love for Juliette overcomes that for her brother. The three women decide to travel on together, posing as sisters, and arrive in Naples, where they engage in atrocious infamies with the king and queen, utilising, as Juliette does more and more frequently, ingenious mechanical contrivances that arithmetically multiply the humiliation and the suffering of her victims. Her passions now require an increasingly technological gratification. Flesh itself is no longer enough.

The girls soon grow bored with Borghese and toss her into the crater of Vesuvius; then they leave Naples, taking with them half the contents of King Ferdinand's treasury, after framing his queen for the theft. But Clairwil's time is running out. It is not that Juliette is growing bored with her too; their affinity is too strong to be eroded by boredom. But the date that the crystal-gazing fortune teller, Durand, forecast for her death is approaching and they meet Durand again, in Ancona, famous for its shrine. Consumed by passion for Juliette, Durand tricks her into poisoning Clairwil and Juliette admits that she, too, is in love with Durand. The two women form a pact of trust, affection and obligation that, henceforward, neither will break.

The form of marriage contract they make between them is an interesting one. Both are murderesses by temperament; they will not even promise that they will not kill one another, however, for such a denial would, in itself, imply a lack of trust. Durand, for all her infinite knowledge and power, is a suppliant for Juliette; she is the more in love and she asks Juliette for only one thing – that she, Durand, will always be the mistress of Juliette's heart and, as to her body, she may do with it what she pleases. Juliette, struck by this combination of rationality and sentiment, swears this will be so. They also make complicated arrangements about their shared finances and their travelling plans. Their first adventure together is a spree with a group of sailors to whom they also sell a great quantity of poisons; in the hands of these two women, Eros is not at war with death but in complicity with it. Their second joint venture is a profitable robbery. Then they set out for Venice, where they open a combined brothel and poison dispensary, with Durand posing as Juliette's mother.

In Venice, Durand experiences her unique but potentially

fatal moment of weakness. Representatives of the Serene
Republic ask her to spread a plague throughout the city and,
stunned by the enormity of the crime, she refuses. As soon as
the words are out of her mouth, she knows she is lost. She
warns Juliette to run away, and herself vanishes, with that
magic speed and conclusiveness characteristic of her. Juliette
assumes Durand has been murdered. Once again, Juliette leaves
great wealth behind her but, since Saint Fond is now dead, she
is able to return to France, where she is welcomed by Noirceuil
and establishes herself once again in Paris. All the money she
abandoned there is restored to her. Her travels are at an end;
home life can begin again. She sends for her infant daughter
from Angers; it is time that the child's education began, she has
reached the age of seven. They all leave for the country, to edu-
cate her in the privacy of Noirceuil's country house.

Noirceuil announces that he wishes to indulge in a curious
fancy.

I should like to get married, not once, but twice on the same
day. At ten o clock in the morning, I wish to dress as a
woman and marry a man; at noon, wearing male dress, I
wish to marry a female role homosexual dressed as my
bride . . . I wish, furthermore, to have a woman do the same
as I do, and what other woman but you, Juliette, could take
part in this game? You, dressed as a woman, must marry a
woman dressed as a man at the same ceremony where I,
dressed as a woman, become the wife of a man. Next, dressed
as a man, you will marry another woman wearing female
attire at the same time that I go to the altar to be united in
holy wedlock with a catamite disguised as a girl.

Her own daughter will marry Juliette when Juliette is dressed as a man; Noirceuil will marry a son and then a daughter of his own. The ceremonies are carried out. They are followed by the slaughter of all the children; these sterile marriages produce, not births, but infanticide.

This charade of sexual anarchy, this gross parody of marriage, this demonstration of the relative mutability of gender, with its culmination in child-murder carried out in a maenad frenzy, is Juliette's annihilation of her residual 'femaleness'; it is, psychologically and emotionally, the climax of her career. Although the narrative continues for a few pages more after this extraordinary episode, she herself has reached her apogee and become the type of criminal female libertine who has cauterised the wounds of her own castration and become a source of pure power. Justine's life was a pilgrimage; Juliette's is a battle campaign with, as its final victory, the conquest of all disgust, horror, superstition, prejudice – and finally, humanity.

When she hurls her daughter into the fire, as she does, she is, at last, absolutely free from any lingering traces of the human responses that can only be learned through the society of others who are not accomplices, who are not aspects of the self that confirm the omnipotence of the self. She has indeed attained the lonely freedom of the libertine, which is the freedom of the outlaw, a tautological condition that exists only for itself and is without any meaning in the general context of human life. Sade's irony suggests that only those who make the laws may inherit this freedom; the moral of Juliette's life suggests the paradox of the hangman – in a country where the hangman rules, only the hangman escapes punishment for his crimes.

Juliette lives in a country where the hangman rules. The hangman is God, the king and the law itself; the hangman is the representative of a patriarchal order which is unjust not because such an order specifically oppresses women but because it is oppressive in itself, since it confines power to a single dominant class. Juliette survives and prospers in this country because she has identified all her interests with those of the hangman.

For Noirceuil and not she has been the instigator of this extraordinary game of dressing up and gender transformation, and he is careful to omit certain elaborations that would truly suggest an anarchy of the sexes – that, for example, Juliette, as a man, should marry he himself, as a woman; not for one moment, even in fantasy, could he allow Juliette to act out that kind of class dominance over himself. For all her aggression, in spite of her dominance over others, Juliette remains a contingent being in relation to Noirceuil, her protector. She depends on his approval; she does as he bids, and her final act of defeminisation is prompted and approved by him.

But now she and Noirceuil proceed to dizzying crimes; they poison a well, and spread devastation throughout the province. They are comrades. They exult in their power of distributing death. As a result of throwing in her lot with the hangman, Juliette has become the hangman herself.

Her autobiography in her own words concludes here. Now the narrative reverts to the third person, in order to report the second version of the death of Justine in an objective style. Justine is to die, again, in an atrocious fashion.

A storm rages outside. The company turns its attention to Juliette's weeping sister; she is thrust out into the tempest and at once a thunderbolt enters her mouth and bursts out through her vagina. She is dead. Juliette and her companions laugh to see how the thunderbolt has ravaged her and commit derisory necrophilies upon her corpse. After a few aphorisms on the negative rewards of virtue, they leave her in the rain and return to the house. Nature has killed Justine in a parody of the act of giving birth.

A coach now arrives at the mansion and from it descends, wonder of wonders, Durand, alive and well and, besides, bringing with her all the revenues that Juliette had abandoned in Venice. She escaped death by acceding to the request of the Republic and infecting the city with plague; she stifled her reluctance and asked for Juliette's funds as a bonus payment. The two women embrace; to the joys of wealth they add those of friendship and of passionate attachment.

Now good news rains in from all sides. A courtier arrives from Versailles; Noirceuil has been made Prime Minister and shares his good fortune with his friends, distributing money and offices with a lordly hand. All ends in a splendid banquet and orgy. They return to Paris, to rule the country.

Juliette will continue her glittering career; until, at about the time of her climacteric, she will die, suddenly, like a meteor that is suddenly extinguished.

II DEATH OF THE GODDESS

Justine is the holy virgin; Juliette is the profane whore. If Juliette has notably fewer spiritual great-granddaughters than her sister in the imaginary brothel where ideas of women are sold, then perhaps it serves to show how much in love with the idea of the blameless suffering of women we all are, men and women both. Juliette never pretends to be blameless. On the contrary, she glories in her crimes, especially in their gratuitousness, and eschews guilt as if it were her victims who should be guilty at their stupidity in falling into her clutches. Since she specialises in *realpolitik*, it is not surprising that she is more like a real woman than Justine could ever be, and bequeathed only a now outmoded model – that of the vamp – to the image industry. Her appearances as Miss Stern, or Dolores, Lady of Pain, are role-playing; Miss Stern existed before Juliette and, as a sexually specialised fantasy, is never either more or less with us.

And, shorn of her menacing apparatus of flagellatory machines, poisons and cunt-cracking dildos that suggest men are supererogatory, Juliette stands for the good old virtues of self-reliance and self-help; 'looking after Number One', as we say in Britain. She is an advertisement of the advantages of free enterprise and her successes in business – her gambling houses, brothels and dispensaries thrive, her investments always yield fruitful returns – are so many examples of the benefits of a free market economy. And not only does she illustrate the advantages of self-help but also of mutual aid. Self-reliant as she is, where would Juliette be without the friends who advise her investments, protect her from the law and warn her when the time comes, as it must come sooner or later in the life of every entrepreneur, to cut her losses and flee to the anonymous securities of her Swiss bank account?

Her satiric function, then, is obvious. The prosperity of crime depends on the fiscal morality of a market-place red in tooth and claw. Juliette is equally criminal in all her dealings, financial as well as sexual. She exploits everyone; no one escapes. The methods of her exploitation are the conventional ones. If Justine's image gave birth to several generations of mythically suffering blondes, Juliette's image lies behind the less numinous prospect of a boardroom full of glamorous and sexy lady executives.

Juliette is of the world, worldly. The main chance is her *modus vivendi*. Her sexual affairs are engaged in either for profit or for fun; she is contemptuous, embarrassed by professions of love. When I think of Juliette, when I try to imagine what she might look like in a restaurant or a night club in late twentieth-century London or New York, when I put her behind a red leather desk high up in one of the corporate palaces of multi-national corporations, tetchily telephoning her stockbroker or, most strikingly, interviewing a secretary, male or female, eyeing the applicant with the canny eye of a farmer in the beast market, I see no more resonant image than that of the *Cosmopolitan* girl – hard, bright, dazzling, meretricious. She plays to win, this one; she knows the score. Her femininity is part of the armoury of self-interest.

Juliette's image has less poetic resonance than that of her sister because its heiresses have inherited a modicum of the power available in the world now. She is the token woman in person. Noirceuil told her how it must be so: '. . . intellect, talents, wealth and influence raise some of the weak from the class into which Nature placed them; as soon as these exceptions enter the class of the strong, they acquire all the rights of the strong. Now tyranny, oppression, impunity from the law and the liberal exercise of every crime are fully permitted to them.'

However, Juliette is also something more than this. The suffering sisterhood of imitation Justines all lack the most singular quality of their progenitor, one it is easy to lose sight of among the misfortunes. Fate rains on Justine. For Justine is extraordinarily single-minded. This single-mindedness makes her a rebel against that Fate that mistreats her; she is in revolt, even, against human nature itself, or, rather, against a view of human nature as irredeemably corrupt. Justine would say, as all good revolutionaries have said: 'Even if it is so, then it should not be so', and, though she is too pusillanimous to do anything about it, she never deviates from her frail and lonely stand, from the idea that men and women need not necessarily be wicked. And to think of Juliette perfectly at home in the twentieth century, telephoning call-girls for her company's clients, is to purposely overlook the same single-mindedness that gives the girls their curious family resemblance.

Juliette is single-mindedly destructive. Her careerist efficiency is a mask for her true subversiveness: her enthusiasm for systems, organisation and self-control conceals her intuition for entropy, for the reinstitution of a primal chaos, her passion for volcanoes. The sisters exist in a complex dialectic with one another; the experience of one makes plain the experience of the other. The innocent Justine is punished by a law she believes is just; the crime-soiled Juliette is rewarded because she undermines the notion of justice on which the law is allegedly based.

If Juliette is ruthless with her creditors, her clients and those who foolishly seek charity from her, she is also ruthless with herself. She desecrates everything, including herself. She overcomes all barriers of fear, shame and guilt in the business of her life, of her career of self-enhancement. She is the embodiment of that merciless excess, that overreaching will to absolute power that carries within it the seeds of its own destruction because in this world, unhappily, there are no absolutes. *Justine* is a pilgrimage of the soul in search of God written by an atheist; *Juliette* is a version of Faust written by a man who believed that, if man exists, we do not need to invent the devil.

Juliette, Delbène, Clairwil, Borghese, Charlotte of Naples and the unhistoric Catherine the Great who appears in Brisatesta's narrative are exceptional women, so exceptional it is easy to mistake them for female impersonators. Mary Wollstonecraft remarked that she had been 'led to imagine that the few extraordinary women who have rushed in eccentrical directions out of the orbit prescribed to their sex were *male* spirits, confined by mistake in female frames.' The virility of these demonic whores – they use the word, 'whore', as a term of endearment for one another almost as often as they affectionately call one another 'buggeress' – suggests male appetites; but, since the avidity of the male appetite is a social fiction, their very insatiability is a mark of their feminity. Clairwil, the man-hater, can exhaust the combined pricks of all the inhabitants of the monastery of the Carmelites, since this insatiability has in itself a castratory function. Male sexuality exhausts itself in its exertion; Clairwil unmans men by fucking them and then retires to the inexhaustible arms of her female lovers.

For these women, the living prick and the manufactured dildo are interchangeable. Both are simply sources of pleasure; the body itself, to which the prick is or has been attached, is no more than a machine for the production of sensation. The world of Juliette is a mechanistic one, even if she and her friends are machine-minders rather than machines themselves, although they define their own pleasure in mechanical terms, so much friction, so many concussions of the nerves. They are the recipients of a technological approach to biology which ensures that Juliette herself is living proof that biology is not destiny, since biology may be so easily emended.

Yet Juliette is more technically a woman than her sister because she bears a child. Justine's inability to conceive is evidence of her invulnerable virginity and she never gives a thought to her reproductive function. Juliette, on the contrary, is fertile. The contraceptive techniques of her time, the sponges inserted in the vagina, the suppositories, the evasion of vaginal penetration, are incorporated into her hygiene. If she should prove unlucky, there is the midwife with her long needle and concoctions of juniper. She aborts an inconvenient foetus; but is prepared to bring to term the child who will ensure her inheritance from the Count de Lorsanges, although she abandons and eventually murders this daughter. Neglect and infanticide are the formal imperfections of Juliette's mothering. They render her mothering invalid.

Her acknowledgement of her fecundity and her refusal to conceive transforms both the form and the content of the act of love itself, just as her refusal to act as a mother changes the nature of the fact that she has given birth. Anal intercourse was, at that time, a capital crime in France because it robbed sexuality of its reproductive aspect; therefore Juliette's enthusiasm for buggery is a subversive use of her own reproductive organs. She is happy to ignore them in the pursuit of pleasure, and, to the pleasure of the flesh, she adds the moral pleasure of a sin against God. Each time she offers her backside to a new lover, she commits an irreligious sacrilege.

Sacrilege is essential to these Sadeian women. The Abbess Delbène loves to get herself fucked upon a coffin in a crypt. In the chapel of the Carmelites, Juliette and Clairwil shit upon crucifixes after the wafer and the wine have been inserted in their fundaments, a comprehensive and ingenious blasphemy. In Rome, Braschi, the Pope, buggers Juliette with a consecrated wafer which has been placed on the tip of his prick. Juliette accomplishes a long-cherished ambition in the Vatican; she has desecrated the holiest sanctum of the Roman church and had an instrumental part in buggering the Host Himself, with all the verb's connotations of contempt, violence and anger. She is a little blasphemous guerrilla of demystification in the Chapel.

She uses sex as an instrument of terror; death is more frequently the result of it than birth. She lobs her sex at men and women as if it were a hand grenade; it will always blow up in their faces. She is a token woman in high places; she is engaged in destroying those high places all the time that she is enjoying the pastimes they offer. She engages in murderous orgies with the Pope and then robs him. She will turn on her friend, Borghese, and toss her into the crater of a volcano. When something better offers itself, she views the death of her beloved Clairwil without regret. And, all the time, she is never in less than full control of her physical self and she has chosen infertility as a way of life because she has chosen sexuality as terrorism as a way of life.

Juliette's infertility is not modified by the fact of giving birth because, under her veneer of acquiescence with the law, she subverts that patriarchal and hereditary institution by denying it her use value, that is, her womb, and the nourishment provided by her breasts.

There is a world of difference between a helplessly barren woman and a purposely infertile one. A woman who remains childless in spite of her own wishes may feel herself bereft and uncompleted, a sub-standard product of the assembly line of nature, who is only a passenger in the world because she has been denied a fertility she feels is part and parcel of her own nature. Rack her brains as she might, she cannot think of any other use for a woman except as a breeder; if she cannot breed, what is she to do? She may think fertility is her birthright, the sign of a theoretical womanhood that gives her a hypothetical pre-eminence over men who may seed the human race but cannot, in themselves, nourish it. This theory of maternal superiority is one of the most damaging of all consolatory fictions and women themselves cannot leave it alone, although it springs from the timeless, placeless, fantasy land of archetypes where all the embodiments of biological supremacy live. It puts those women who wholeheartedly subscribe to it in voluntary exile from the historic world, this world, in its historic time that is counted out minute by minute, in which no event or circumstance of life exists for itself but is determined by an interlocking web of circumstances, where actions achieve effects and my fertility is governed by my diet, the age at which I reached puberty, my bodily juices, my decisions – not by any benevolent magics.

Because she is the channel of life, woman as mythic mother lives at one remove from life. A woman who defines herself through her fertility has no other option. So a woman who feels she has been deprived of motherhood is trebly deprived – of children; of the value of herself as mother; and of her own self, as autonomous being.

But a woman who has chosen infertility does not feel this deprivation. All the same, she is not a surrogate man. By no means. All of her, her breasts, her cunt, her innards, are perfectly female – perhaps more perfectly so, from the point of view of aesthetics, than those of a woman who has borne children. But the significance of these things is completely altered.

We are living in a period where this alteration of significance is under debate in a variety of ways. Techniques of contraception and surgically safe abortion have given women the choice to be sexually active yet intentionally infertile for more of their lives than was possible at any time in history until now. This phenomenon is most apparent in those industrialised countries where the social position of women has been a subject of dissension since the late eighteenth century and the beginning of the industrial revolution; indeed, the introduction of contraception is part of the change in the position of women over the last two centuries. But all this speculation does not seem to have lessened the shock of the psychic impact of the division between the female body and the fact of child-bearing. It ought to seem self-evident that this body need not necessarily bear children but the trace-effects of several millennia during which this fact was not self-evident at all, since it was continually obscured by enforced pregnancies, have clothed the female body almost inpenetrably with a kind of mystification, of kitschification, that removes it almost from the real or physiological fact.

Consider the womb, the 'inner productive space', as Erik Erikson calls it, the extensible realm sited in the penetrable flesh, most potent matrix of all mysteries. The great, good place; domain of futurity in which the embryo forms itself from the flesh and blood of its mother; the unguessable reaches of the sea are a symbol of it, and so are caves, those dark, sequestered places where initiation and revelation take place. Men long for it and fear it; the womb, that comfortably elastic organ, is a fleshly link between past and future, the physical location of an everlasting present tense that can usefully serve as a symbol of eternity, a concept that has always presented some difficulties in visualisation. The hypothetical dream-time of the foetus seems to be the best that we can do.

For men, to fuck is to have some arcane commerce with this place of ultimate privilege, where, during his lengthy but unre-membered stay, he was nourished, protected, lulled to sleep by the beating of his mother's heart and not expected to do a stroke of work, a repose, of course, not unlike that of a corpse, except that a foetus's future lies before it. And the curious resemblance between the womb and the grave lies at the roots of all human ambivalence towards both the womb and its bearer; we mediate our experience through imagination and dream but sometimes the dream gets in the way of the experi-ence, and obscures it completely – the womb is the First and Last Place, earth, the greatest mother of them all, from whom we come, to whom we go. (Unless we more hygienically decide to resolve ourselves to fire – imagery, however, from a different religious structure than that of Western European culture and difficult to reconcile with it. It will be a long time before the idea of the crematorium transcends its pedestrian function, that of burning corpses, and becomes as numinous as the graveyard.

The womb is the earth and also the grave of being; it is the warm, moist, dark, inward, secret, forbidden, fleshly core of the unknowable labyrinth of our experience. Curiously, it is the same for both men and women, because the foetus is either male or female, though sometimes both; but only men are supposed to feel a holy dread before its hairy portals. Only men are privileged to return, even if only partially and intermittently, to this place of fleshly extinction; and that is why they have a better grasp of eternity and abstract concepts than we do.

They want it for themselves, of course. But not, of course, a real one, with all the mess and inconvenience that goes with it. The womb is an imaginative locale and has an imaginative location far away from my belly, beyond my flesh, beyond my house, beyond this city, this society, this economic structure – it lies in an area of psychic metaphysiology suggesting such an anterior primacy of the womb that our poor dissecting tools of reason blunt on its magnitude before they can even start on the job. This inner space must have been there before any of the outer places; in the beginning was the womb and its periodic and haphazard bleedings are so many signs that it has a life of its own, unknowable to us. This is the most sacred of all places. Women are sacred because they possess it. That, as Justine would have known if she had thought about it, is why they are treated so badly for nothing can defile the sacred.

Sade's invention of Juliette is an emphatic denial of this entrancing rhetoric. For rhetoric it is, compounded out of several millennia of guesses and fantasies about the nature of the world. The truth of the womb is, that it is an organ like any other organ, more useful than the appendix, less useful than the colon but not much use to you at all if you do not wish to utilise its sole function, that of bearing children. At the best of times, it is apt to malfunction and cause sickness, pain and inconvenience. The assertion of this elementary fact through the means of a fictional woman involves an entire process of demystification and denial, in which far more than the demystification, the secularisation of women is involved.

To deny the bankrupt enchantments of the womb is to pare a good deal of the fraudulent magic from the idea of women, to reveal us as we are, simple creatures of flesh and blood whose expectations deviate from biological necessity sufficiently to force us to abandon, perhaps regretfully, perhaps with relief, the deluded priestesshood of a holy reproductive function. This demystification extends to the biological iconography of women.

The breasts remain, but must be encountered, now, as breasts, not as the balcony of the goddess from whence she magisterially addresses her devotees in a metalanguage of self-adulation. They are no longer the general rendezvous of love and hunger, inspiring a Pavlovian response of need, but the specific breasts of a specific woman. One must not generalise about any breasts any more. To generalise is to lose the woman to whom they belong. They may remind both men and women of their own mother's breasts but these were also the lactatory glands of a specific woman and in her specificness alone resides their significance. Inside the belly, the womb, the ovaries and the Fallopian tubes remain; however, the ovaries and the Fallopian tubes have never, for some reason, been enriched with such a queasy burden of overvaluation as the womb, although childbearing would be impossible without them. All this apparatus remains; but a voluntary sterility, freely chosen, makes them of as little and as great significance as any other part of the human body without which it is possible to survive.

The goddess is dead.

And, with the imaginary construct of the goddess, dies the notion of eternity, whose place on this earth was her womb. If the goddess is dead, there is nowhere for eternity to hide. The last resort of homecoming is denied us. We are confronted with mortality, as if for the first time.

There is no way out of time. We must learn to live in this world, to take it with sufficient seriousness, because it is the only world that we will ever know.

I think this is why so many people find the idea of the emancipation of women frightening. It represents the final secularisation of mankind. The old joke of the early sixties – the astronaut, returning from heaven, describes God: 'This may come as a bit of a shock, but *she's black*' – was a last queasy attempt to put something transcendental, at least up there, even if the Supreme Being was doubly devalued, by virtue of Her sex and Her race. With the death of the goddess go the last shreds of the supernatural. With apologies to Appollinaire, I do not think I want Juliette to renew my world; but, her work of destruction complete, she will, with her own death, have removed a repressive and authoritarian superstructure that has prevented a good deal of the work of renewal. For Juliette, secularised as she is, is in the service of the goddess, too, even if of the goddess in her demonic aspect, the goddess as antithesis.

III THE PHALLIC MOTHER

Durand is in her late forties. She has arrived at post-menopausal sterility and exists purely as a being of flesh and reason. She cannot reproduce, even if she wanted to. This is also the condition of the four brilliant whores who survive the holocaust at the Castle of Silling in *The Hundred and Twenty Days at Sodom*, women whose intellectual rapacity and sexual omnivorousness is the equal of that of Juliette and her friends. All these women are well past the age of child-bearing and child-bearing has never been a major factor in their lives. For preference, the whores, Madame Champville, Madame Martaine, Madame Duclos and Madame Desgranges, utilise the anus, the unisexual orifice; that of Madame Desgranges, in particular, has become extremely capacious through use. Sin and contraception aside, anal intercourse has an egalitarian lure for Sade. If sexual relations are implicitly political in Sade, the sexual act, among equals, is one of mutual if sequential dominance. Now the woman, now the man, penetrates and is penetrated in turn; gender itself can become interchangeable, as in the sexual charade that concludes Juliette's career. The homosexual de Bressac told Justine how much he enjoyed becoming a woman for the purposes of sex; Dolmancé, the erotic tutor in *Philosophy in the Boudoir*, enjoys experiencing his anus as a vagina. The female libertines, as Zarathustra recommended, never forget their whips when visiting; but they never leave behind their dildos, either.

And the four whores in *The Hundred and Twenty Days at Sodom* are more virile, in many respects, than the libertines who employ them. Durcet, the banker, with his vestigial tits and soft buttocks, is a singularly equivocal figure. But Madame Champville has a clitoris capable of erecting itself three inches, the extent of Durcet's own erection. This flexible clitoris-cum-prick is in ironic contrast to some of the pricks of the male sexual slaves at the Castle, which are of such a size that they cannot penetrate a woman at all, and are so many meaningless appendages, signs of a masculinity so gross it exceeds its own purpose.

Erectile clitorida are a feature of Sade's tribades; they are reminiscent in this respect of certain African tribeswomen whose labia minora and clitorida are artificially elongated until they resemble male genitals. Volmar, an inhabitant of the convent where Juliette was educated, is equipped with a three-inch-long clitoris that enables her to penetrate other women both vaginally and anally; of voracious sexual appetites, she must either be a nymphomaniac or a sodomite or else cease to fuck at all. By exercising a Sadeian right to fuck, she automatically flies in the face of Nature whatever she does.

Durand is the queen of all these androgynes. She is 'the most remarkable libertine of her century'. She is handsome, with superb breasts, an enormous clitoris and an obstruction of the vagina which has prevented her from ever engaging in orthodox heterosexual intercourse in all her life. The way to her womb is blocked.

Though she cannot make babies, she can make corpses. 'She takes a box out of her pocket and sprinkles the cemetery with the powder the box contained' relates Juliette. 'All at once, the ground was scattered with corpses.' These magical performances suggest that Durand is beginning to approach the strangeness of an anti-myth of mothering. In the place of a reproductive function, she has acquired an absolute mastery of the physical world. She has exchanged motherhood for domination. 'All Nature obeys my orders, because she always submits herself to the will of those who uncover her secrets,' she tells Juliette. She is a scientist; it is the discipline of the scientific method that has brought her to this pitch.

If she could but lay her hands on the one poison plant she knows would do the trick, she has the ability to destroy the entire earth; she is the ecological crisis in person. She can propagate epidemics; poison wells; slaughter cattle; destroy villages; infect the Republic of Venice with a fatal plague. She has invented an entire pharmacopoeia of poisons and, if she procures a handsome profit from their sale, she is also moved in her research by an impulse of pure misanthropy. She would like, she confides to Juliette, to destroy everything.

In her house, the rich immolate the poor with the aid of baroque machinery, amongst picturesque decors similar to those of the ballets of the period. She is a choreographer of life and death. And, although she works her macabre miracles with the aid of science, she has about her a theatrical whiff of black magic. Her laboratory and her garden of venomous plants are those of the medieval alchemist and the witch-herbalist. She calls up sylphs and spirits with incantatory formulae. She practises divination, the antique practice of woman as oracle and seer; a mother-figure is reproduced in the form of a goddess of destiny in Jean Thenaud's sixteenth-century *Traité de la Cabale*, yet Durand derives much of her style from the fashionable necromancy of the late eighteenth century. She is both a cabalistic enigma and *diabolism à la mode*.

Juliette falls in love with her at first sight when she meets her in Paris; but, the next time Juliette visits Durand's house, the windows are shuttered, it is deserted. No matter how hard she tries, she cannot find out what has become of the sorceress, who has vanished with a magic and complete precipitation, to reappear again just as mysteriously in Italy. Even though she has been condemned to death, Durand will magically resurrect herself to crown Juliette's final good fortune; her capacity for appearance and disappearance exceeds even the generous limits of the picaresque novel so that, for all her invocations of science, her outlines are subtly blurred with the supernatural even if the god she invokes for Juliette and Clairwil turns out to be a mortal phallus.

She treats science as if it were magic. She uses her discoveries for personal gratification and for financial profit, just as Dr Faustus in Marlowe's play did with the powers for which he exchanged his soul. She has made, of forbidden knowledge, a service industry.

However, the more one examines this ambivalent and terrifying woman, the more unreal she becomes, the more like a reformulation of the goddess in the terms of a different reading of her iconography. Durand comes to resemble a mother indeed, but not the adult sentimentalisation of the memory of the protective mother; rather, she is the omnipotent mother of early childhood who gave and withheld love and nourishment at whim, as it seemed to us. The cruel mother, huge as a giantess, the punishment giver, the one who makes you cry.

But Durand, final terror, is not only infertile but also unapproachable; she may not be entered by the antechamber of the womb. She is therefore unappeasable.

It is as if the milk from her superb breasts had been transformed into poisons when Nature imperiously denied access to her interior. The ambiguous affirmation of Durand's breasts recalls the fantasies of the small boys described by Bruno Bettelheim, who believed that women could suckle themselves.

These boys were envious of breasts independently of lactation, says Bettelheim; they viewed them as sources of strength and power in themselves.

This power is perilous. Durand is like a version of the Terrible Mother, the Hindu goddess, Kali, who stands for both birth and death, and not only destruction but Nature's cruel indifference to suffering. Clairwil and Juliette, like Tantric devotees of Kali, engage in sexual rituals in a graveyard, at Durand's instigation. Kali herself dances upon severed heads, juggles with limbs, wears necklaces of skulls and copulates with corpses. Snakes issue from her vulva.

Durand is as destructive as Kali, a sumptuous infecundity whose masterpieces are plagues.

In Durand, the Enlightenment returns to pure mythology. Reason overreaches itself and turns into the opposite of reason. Scientific order, ruthlessly applied, reduces the world to chaos. Durand, the rational biochemist, is the very mythic terror that reason fears most.

But her mothering passion for Juliette serves to reassure us that her ambivalence is inconsistent and, though she has an infinite capacity for destruction, she will not use her poisons and magics against us, whom she loves. If Durand's penetrable vagina, the road back to the solace of the womb, is inaccessible, that is because it has been turned inside out, has become the clitoris that Juliette, when she first sees it, at once begins to suck, as though it were a teat.

Durand is a virile and non-productive mother, who chooses her own children and seduces them, too. She is a mother with a phallus; she can rape even nature itself. The dead goddess resurrects herself in the form of her antithesis, not as cherishing and nourishment but absence and hunger. Or, rather, as cherishing for some and absence for others.

But Juliette has Durand's promise this mother will never desert her. Unlike Justine, Juliette is not an orphan in the world. She is intimately related to the origins of chaos and so she will be protected from it, until it repossesses her.

FOUR

The School of Love:
The Education of a Female Oedipus

> The aggressive impulses of little girls leave nothing to be desired
> in the way of abundance and violence.
> *New Introductory Lectures in Psychoanalysis, No. Three:*
> *'Femininity'*, Sigmund Freud

I MOTHERS AND DAUGHTERS

Philosophy in the Boudoir is not a picaresque epic novel. It is a dramatic interlude, on a very much smaller scale than the novels and very much less cluttered and repetitious in style. Its manner is intimate and domestic, its setting a boudoir as elegant and civilised as those in the pictures of Watteau and Fragonard. The characters, with the exception of a gardener, are all of Sade's own class and the atmosphere of the piece has the elegant depravity of Laclos's *Les Liaisons Dangereuses*. If, outside, they are selling pamphlets on the steps of the Palace of Equality, inside, in the privileged boudoir, the ladies and gentlemen still pleasure themselves at leisure.

At the conclusion of *Philosophy in the Boudoir*, a young girl, Eugénie de Mistival, commits a gross sexual assault upon her mother. Though it is performed with obscene relish, this monstrous act is primarily occasioned by vengeance, rather than lust. The girl rapes her mother because the woman has attempted to curtail Eugénie's sexual experience. The woman who does not wish to permit others to engage in sexual activity for the sake of pleasure must herself have sex inflicted on her as retribution, as a form of punishment uniquely fitted for her crime against pleasure.

Eugénie, however, goes much further than a simple rape. She first rapes her and then sews up her mother's genital orifice with needle and thread, as though she must effectively annihilate her mother's sexuality before she herself can be free. It would seem that, in some sense, her mother's sexuality menaces her own. The mother wishes Eugénie to behave as if her sexual organs were sealed and therefore Eugénie seals up her mother, to remove the possibility of rivalry, the only reason her mother might possibly have to wish to repress her daughter's sexuality.

King Oedipus' transgressions were mother-incest and parricide; when he found out what he had done, he blinded himself, that is, underwent a symbolic castration. Eugénie, unlike Oedipus, acts in the knowledge she is committing a crime. Her crime is the culmination of her search for knowledge. She fucks her mother out of vengeance and so finds herself in the position of a female Oedipus but she is not blinded, she is enlightened; then, in spite and rage, she seals up the organs of generation that bore her and so ensures that her mother will not fuck again with anyone.

Philosophy in the Boudoir is a detailed account of the erotic education of a Sadeian heroine. The basis of the plot is Eugénie's relation to her mother and her final ambivalent triumph over the female principle as typified in the reproductive function. The mother has burst angrily into the profane academy, the school of love, during her daughter's initiation in order to rescue her daughter from sexual experience; her punishment is rape, infection and infibulation.

The narrative, composed in a series of seven dialogues in dramatic form, begins when Eugénie, fifteen years old, arrives at the boudoir of Madame de Saint-Ange, her libertine father's mistress, eager for instruction. Innocence is not her quality. She is already engaged in a lesbian affair with Saint-Ange. But she is ignorant and has come to the older woman to be instructed, with her father's knowledge, against her mother's wishes. Saint-Ange intends to spare nothing to 'pervert her, degrade her, demolish in her all the false ethical notions with which they [her mother's friends] have been able to dull her.'

The voluptuous Saint-Ange, a widow of twenty-six, has employed as fellow tutors her brother, the Chevalier de Mirvel, and the libertine Dolmancé. Dolmancé, a lover of the Chevalier, has succumbed to Saint-Ange's invitation only in order to take the opportunity of sodomising her; he refuses to approach women by any other orifice than the unnatural one. He will preside over Saint-Ange's little academy. The course will encompass both theory and practice. Saint-Ange intends her brother to depucelate Eugénie's frontal orifice, Dolmancé to deal with her anus. These deflorations are duly performed, to Eugénie's delight.

Saint-Ange and the cynical Dolmancé share that sensual rapacity which is the mark of the Sadeian libertine. The

Chevalier, though equally adroit sexually, yet retains a sense of the injustice of their voluptuous privilege, and, curiously enough, is not punished for announcing this, although his sermon is ignored. It is he who will introduce politics into the lessons. But the purpose of the gathering is primarily this: to strip Eugénie of all her socialised virtues and to restore her to the primal and vicious state of nature. Her education has regression rather than maturation as its goal.

She is given an anatomy lesson in which Saint-Ange's body serves as a blackboard. She is instructed in the function of the clitoris and told that all a woman's powers of sensation lie there. Dolmancé's prick and balls are demonstrated to her and she is taught how to masturbate him. The physiology of sex, however, takes up very little of their time. The strenuous and protracted orgies, conducted with military precision and clockwork timing, are punctuated by philosophical sermons on the family, on marriage, contraception, abortion, prostitution, cruelty and love. The virile and handsome gardener joins them for some of the sexual activity but he is prudently ordered out of the room while Chevalier reads aloud the political pamphlet: *Yet Another Effort, Frenchmen, if you Would Become Republican.* This pamphlet occupies between a third and a half of the text of the entire piece. During the revolution of 1848, it was extracted from its pornographic context and republished by the followers of the Utopian, Saint-Simon.

The opinions expressed in it are republican and atheist; they are the blueprints for a society where the laws are 'so mild, so few, that all men, whatever their character, can easily keep them'. In this society, women are held in common; but also hold men in common.

138

If we admit . . . that all women should submit to our desires, surely we ought also to allow them to fully satisfy their own . . . Charming sex, you will be free; just as men do, you shall enjoy all the pleasures that Nature makes your duty, do not withhold yourselves from one. Must the diviner part of mankind be kept in chains by the other? Ah, break those bonds; nature wills it. Have no other curb than your tastes, no other laws than those of your own desires, no more morality than that of Nature herself. Languish no more under those barbarous prejudices that wither your charms and imprison the divine impulses of your heart: you are as free as we are and the career of the battles of Venus as open to you as to us.

Sade does not concern himself with problems of capital investment or economic organisation in the hypothetical republic; those are not his areas of concern. He is concerned to forge a libertarian sexuality and the libertines listen with approval. Eugénie's education will take this lesson into account; if it does not leave her in possession of the liberty the pamphlet attempts to describe, then she will go out into the world in possession of a certain qualified freedom, the most the historical circumstances of the time can offer. This qualified freedom may not be attained without a process similar to an initiation. Almost as soon as she arrives in the boudoir, she gives us a clue as to who it is who must be sacrificed before her initiation is complete.

EUGÉNIE: . . . every day I see before me an abominable creature I've wanted in her grave for years.
SAINT-ANGE: I think I can guess who that might be.

EUGÉNIE: Who do you suspect?
SAINT-ANGE: Your mother?
EUGÉNIE: Oh, let me hide my blushes in your bosom !

Eugénie's tutors apply rational science to the discussion of this antipathy. Since rationality is also relative, the science to which they refer is, in fact, incorrect. Saint-Ange opines that, because 'the foetus owes its existence only to the man's sperm', filial tenderness is naturally reserved entirely for the father. This theory was general scientific currency of the period. The animalculists, or spermists, who believed the spermatozoa were of more significance than the ova in the process of conception, had returned to the classical theory of Aeschylus: the parent is the male, the mother only 'the nurse of the young life that is sown within her'. This devaluation of the actual biological status of women indicates how far prejudice can invalidate certain scientific theorising before it even begins. On this biological misinterpretation, Sade builds an edifice of mother-hatred.

DOLMANCÉ: I am not yet consoled for my father's death; when I lost my mother, I lit a perfect bonfire for joy . . . formed uniquely out of the blood of our fathers, we owe nothing at all to our mothers. All they did was to co-operate in the act which our fathers urged them to. So, it was the father who desired our birth; the mother only consents to it.

There is no virtue in the accidental creativity of the mother since fecundity itself is not a necessary part of the natural scheme of things, says Sade. Nature does not urge procreation but merely tolerates it; Saint-Ange urges Eugénie to avoid conception by whatever means she can. However, once the homunculus has been deposited within a woman, she herself is in sole charge of it. Now she may exercise a free choice as to what she intends to do with it. 'We are always mistress of what we carry in our womb,' says Saint-Ange. She must not dread the idea of abortion, if that is what she so wishes. (Attempted abortion and infanticide were both capital crimes in France at the time, also.)

Sade is content to deny any significance to the activity of the physical mother beyond the fact of the ripening of the embryo in her body. Since he seeks a complete divorce between sexuality and reproduction, he does not see any value in physical mothering at all. Moral mothering, the care and education of children, is a different matter and should be left to those who have shown themselves competent at it; besides, if the sexual liberty he wishes to see in the Republic is put into practice, legitimacy will cease to be a legal fact and the nuclear family itself will wither away. Further, one must take into account the child, whose existence is Mother's sole claim to distinction in the world. The existence of the child is essential to the notion of motherhood but the child has had even less choice in the matter than its mother has. In this enforced and involuntary relationship, how can mother and child be anything but enemies? Especially when a girl child grasps the fact of her mother's passive acquiescence in her conception, and, in Freudian terms, realises that her mother is castrated?

Let Eugénie, then, savagely restore to her mother the phallus she lacks, mocking her mother's gratuitous fecundity with a mechanical implement that will not fecundate her. Eugénie will fuck her with a cunt-cracking dildo. 'Come, dear lovely Mama, come, let me treat you like a husband.' Eugénie takes on the sexual aggressiveness of her father by mimicking her father; she exhibits a naive triumph at the speed and completeness with which she has superseded the condition of female passivity to which she had been trained.

As Dolmancé penetrates her anally while she inflicts the artificial penis with which he has equipped her upon her mother, Eugénie cries: 'Here I am, at one stroke incestuous, adultress, sodomite and all that in a girl who has only lost her virginity today!' The act of profanation and sacrilege she has performed, a fugue of sexual and familial misconduct, is a Sadeian *rite de passage* into complete sexual being. The violence of Eugénie's reaction is some indication of the degree of repression from which she has suffered. It is also a characteristic piece of Sadeian black humour.

Then the libertines invalidate Madame de Mistival's long-cherished and hypocritical chastity by introducing into the gathering a syphilitic who inoculates her with the pox in both orifices, forcing her to suffer the very punishment specially reserved by natural justice for the pleasures she has always denied herself. Finally, Eugénie seizes needle and thread and sews her securely up. Then, to complete the exemplary humiliation, we will assure her we have her husband's, our father's, full approval of all the infamies we have committed and drive her from our bedroom, the abode of unrepressed sexuality, an inverted Eden beyond the knowledge of good and evil, a dark Beulah where contrarities exist together, with abuse and blows.

DOLMANCÉ: Let this example serve to remind you that your
daughter is old enough to do what she wants; that she
loves to fuck, that she was born to fuck, and that, if you
do not wish to be fucked yourself, at least you can leave
her alone.

But before the mother goes, she must beg her daughter's pardon
for attempting to repress her. Eugénie's delirious transgression
has ensured her own sexual freedom at the cost of the violent
cessation of the possibility of her mother's own sexual life. Her
triumph over her mother is complete.

The relation between Eugénie and her mother is an extreme
and melodramatised, indeed, pornographised description of the
antipathy between mothers and daughters which suggests that
women, also, retain elements of the early erotic relation with
the mother that has been more fully explored and documented
in men. Indeed, *Philosophy in the Boudoir* in many ways precedes
Freud's essay on femininity, and should be seen in the same
Western European context of competition and rivalry between
women that devalues women as they act them out in the
dramas of sexual life. But Sade is not engaged in the exposition
of fact but of fantasy, of symbolic sexual interaction, and his
version of the conflict between mother and daughter may be
interpreted like this: the mother wishes to repress her growing
daughter's sexuality because she herself is growing old and social
custom is removing her from the arena of sexual life. She sees
her daughter, the living memory of herself as a young woman, as
both an immediate rival and a poignant reminder of what she
herself is losing. The daughter, on the other hand, sees the
mother, not as an ageing rival but as a mature woman and one

in permanent possession of her father, who is the most immediately present object on which she may focus her desire. Not only is the mother the rival of the daughter but her position as wife of the father is impregnable. Sexual hostility is therefore the inevitable relation between mother and daughter, as long as the mother regards sexuality as synonymous with reproduction and hence sanctified activity in which only the Holy Mother, herself, may indulge. Saint-Ange, as instructress, adopts another kind of maternal role towards Eugénie, as Durand does towards Juliette. But no natural mother in Sade is capable of this, because she is a shrine of reproductive sexuality. She is herself the embodiment of the repression of sexual pleasure; how, then, can she not attempt to repress sexuality in her daughter?

Mother is in herself a concrete denial of the idea of sexual pleasure since her sexuality has been placed at the service of reproductive function alone. She is the perpetually violated passive principle; her autonomy has been sufficiently eroded by the presence within her of the embryo she brought to term. Her unthinking ability to reproduce, which is her pride, is, since it is beyond choice, not a specific virtue of her own. The daughter may achieve autonomy only through destroying the mother, who represents her own reproductive function, also, who is both her own mother and the potential mother within herself.

If the daughter is a mocking memory to the mother – 'As I am, so you once were' – then the mother is a horrid warning to her daughter. 'As I am, so you will be.' Mother seeks to ensure the continuance of her own repression, and her hypocritical solicitude for the younger woman's moral, that is, sexual welfare masks a desire to reduce her daughter to the same state of contingent passivity she herself inhabits, a state honoured by custom and hedged by taboo.

Vengeance. Transgression. Glory! Eugénie de Mistival offers her arse to her mother and invites her to kiss it. Her seizure of her own autonomy necessitates the rupture of all the taboos she can apprehend. She will take her mother to wife and symbolically kill her, too; and the conflict is solely between women. Father, though continually invoked, is absent from this malign fiesta, just as he is absent from every child's primary experience, the birth and the breast, the first bed and the first table. Eugénie and her companions, her playmates, are alone with Eugénie's first beloved and first seducer and may wreak upon her a suitable vengeance for her betrayal.

Baby is hermaphrodite. It is polysexual. It is all the sexes in one and first of all it will love the thing that feeds and caresses it, out of necessity. During this period, father is only a troublesome rival for the attention of the mother. Freud suggests that the relation with the mother regularly structures a woman's relation with her father. Adult women with particularly strong attachments to their fathers had usually, he suggests, transferred a peculiarly strong first passion for the mother to the father in all its entirety and intensity. This primal passion has necessarily been libidinal and will have passed through all the oral, sadistic, and phallic phases of infantile sexuality; it will be essentially ambivalent, now affectionate, now hostile. There will be fantasies of making the mother pregnant and of becoming pregnant by the mother. Mother and daughter live as each one the other's image.

In the Freudian orchestration, now father enters the nursery and interposes his phallic presence between his daughter and her mother; his arrival in the psychic theatre, bearing his irreplaceable prick before him like a wand of office, a conductor's baton, a sword of severance, signifies the end of the mother's role as seducer and as beloved. 'The turning away from the mother is accompanied by hostility; the attachment to the mother ends in hate,' hypothesises Freud in his essay on femininity in the *New Introductory Lectures in Psychoanalysis*. The primary passion was incapable of the consummation of a child. The girl now turns to the father in the expectation he will give her the object that he possesses which she lacks, the phallus that is a substitute child and also makes children, that weapon which is a symbol of authority, of power, and will pierce the opacity of the world. Freud's account of this process has such extraordinary poetic force that, however false it might be, it remains important as an account of what seemed, at one point in history, a possible progression. It retains a cultural importance analagous, though less far-reaching, to the myth of the crime of Eve in the Old Testament.

Now Eugénie obeys the Freudian scenario as if she were one of his patients. She seeks the aid of a man, even if Saint-Ange, her surrogate mother, has adequately endowed her with aggression and competently seduced her, too. But Dolmancé, the ambiguous schoolmaster, the Tiresias who loves to play the woman and scrupulously avoids cunts, presses into Eugénie's hand a false limb, a dildo, and suggests a parodic accomplishment of the first desire of all, an act of sexual aggression that will exorcise the desire for good and all. So Eugénie 'plays the husband' to her lovely Mama, acts out upon the mirror image of her own flesh a charade of domination and possession.

In the terms of a theory of sexuality that denies any significance to reproduction, such as Sade's, the castrate is the human
norm. If Eugénie, a typically Freudian girl, suffers a typically
Freudian penis-envy, then it is amply compensated for by the
acquisition of a mechanical device that is just as good a phallus
as a real one could ever be. When Clairwil in *Juliette* mastur-
bates with a mummified penis, the penis becomes an object,
dissociated from any human context. It is no longer a symbol of
malehood. It is 'the sceptre of Venus', 'the primary agent of
love's pleasure', and may be wielded by whomsoever chooses to
do so, regardless of the bearer's gender.

Eugénie penetrates her mother. Madame de Mistival faints.
Eugénie hopes she has not died because she had already
planned her summer wardrobe; what a bore it would be to have
to abandon all her pretty frocks and put on mourning instead!
Even her tutors are taken aback at that; she has already sur-
passed her masters in the art of hardening her heart. Then
Dolmancé whips the woman awake with freshly gathered
thorns while his companions perform a sprightly erotic tableau
and achieve orgasm in well-choreographed unison. Each actor
then pronounces judgement upon the vanquished mother.
Eugénie, most vicious since most in love, would like to drive
whips tipped with sulphur into her mother's body and set fire to
them. But Dolmancé, the most cerebral, has a better idea; it is
he who introduces the syphilitic, who will inject his poison into
Madame de Mistival's vagina and anus 'with this consequence:
that so long as this cruel disease's impressions shall last, the
whore will remember not to trouble her daughter when Eugénie
has herself fucked.'

Everyone applauds the scheme. It is carried out immediately, while the others vigorously whip one another. Then Saint-Ange, the surrogate or adoptive mother, suggests Eugénie sew her natural mother up, to prevent the infection leaking out of her.

EUGÉNIE: Excellent idea! Quickly, quickly, fetch me needle and thread! . . . Spread your thighs, Mama, so I can stitch you together – so that you'll give me no more little brothers and sisters.

The child ceases to love Mother when the arrival of siblings puts its nose out of joint for good. Eugénie's delirium is now in a fugal flood where innumerable themes play together; but jealousy and the desire for revenge are uppermost. Mother must be punished because her passivity invites action; humiliated, because of her pride; raped, in order violently to restore to her the penis which she lacks; infected, to mock her chastity; rendered incapable of reproduction, because she has sanctified her fecundity.

And all these villainies must be heaped upon her unwilling but helplessly compliant body because it could not accommodate the impossible demands for absolute love that the child, her everlastingly unrequited suitor, made upon it. So Mama leaves the School of Love and the Chevalier, who takes her home, is warned to keep his hands off her, since she has the pox. She has learned that her daughter is old enough to do as she pleases, that her attempts at sexual restraint have proved worse than useless, have provoked the most violent reaction, have destroyed her.

And perhaps Mama has been enlightened; but not so far enlightened that Sade will let her stay to join in the fun.

'Mothers,' thunders Sade in the preface of the first edition, 'prescribe this book to your daughters!' In the second edition, however, he changes his tune. He vacillates. He warns: 'Mothers, proscribe this book to your daughters.' But perhaps this is a printing error; by the time the second edition was printed, Sade had been interred in the asylum at Charenton and had no control over the proofs. Nevertheless, the vowels slip into and out of one another. Prescribe. Proscribe. What to do, what to do.

He acknowledges to the full the mutual antagonism between mother and daughter. But should the mother or the daughter be enlightened as to the nature and extent of this antagonism? Which one of them should have the benefit of the lesson? Or should they both?

Eugénie's libido thrusts her towards an attack upon the female orifice itself, which is an implicit attack upon her own biological function. But it is an attack, a rape, not a ravishment. She never contemplates a seduction, even though she eroticises her mother when she fucks her. She opens her up for pleasure with the massive dildo. 'I believe, dear Mother, you are coming . . . Dolmancé, look at her eyes! She comes, it's certain.' At this point, Madame de Mistival decides to lose consciousness and so censor her own situation. In other words, Sade has scared himself so badly by the obvious resolution of the psychodrama that he has set his creators to act out that he decides to censor her response. It frightens him. So Madame de Mistival must deny responsibility even for her own responses. She will experience sexuality like a theft from herself.

Neither she, nor Eugénie, nor Dolmancé, nor even Saint-Ange, nor, especially, Sade, can tolerate the implication of her orgasm. 'She comes, it's certain!' But this is Eugénie's vicious mockery; Mother must never be allowed to come, and so to come alive. She cannot be corrupted into the experience of sexual pleasure and so set free. She is locked forever in the fortress of her flesh, a sleeping beauty whose lapse of being is absolute and eternal. If she were allowed to taste one single moment's pleasure in the abuses that are heaped upon her, abuses that would glut Saint-Ange or her own daughter with joy, that would overthrow the whole scheme.

Vice and virtue, that is, energy and passivity, that is, evil and good, would then be states to which one could accede. As it is, in the model of the world that Sade has made, a man or a woman is naturally vicious or naturally virtuous; Eugénie is already corrupt when she arrives at Saint-Ange's boudoir, Juliette was already wicked when she registered at Delbène's academy. Sade's manicheistic dualism sees the world as irredeemably evil; vice must always prosper, virtue always despair. There is no hope for us as we are now. The Republic in which the laws 'are as mild as the people they govern' is as much a fantasy as Saint-Ange's voluptuous boudoir. Sade's vision is utterly without transcendence. But, if he could have allowed himself to violate the last taboo of all, and allow wretched and abused Madame de Mistival to experience pleasure, then the terms of his vision would be disrupted. Transcendence would have crept in. He might even have to make room for hope.

Being would cease to be a state-in-itself; it would then be possible to move between modes of being in a moral and not a sexual sense. By denying the possibility of corruption, Sade denies the possibility of regeneration.

The possibility of the redemption from virtue would suggest the reciprocal possibility of a fall from vice.

But Madame de Mistival, if she does indeed feel the first faint prick of pleasure, faints to avoid the consciousness of it. They rouse her from the faint only to sew her up. Then she is infected and now she is impregnable. She no longer coexists with even the possibility of pleasure. She is better than dead.

Now we are beginning to approach the central paradox of all Sade's pornography, which is inherent in the paradox of his own sexuality.

Sade, contemplating the phallus, real or artificial, dithers. Let us prescribe it to our daughters, by all means. But he cannot finally decide whether it is an instrument of pleasure, pure and simple, as it might be in the Republic, where women are 'common fountains of pleasure', or a weapon of admonition, pure and simple, as it is for Eugénie, for Clairwil and his male libertines.

He himself has always wanted one. He wanted his mother's phallus but it transpired she had none to give him; if Freud is correct and boy children regularly endow all the other beings in the world with the appendage they themselves possess, the shock and grief of the discovery that the mother lacks one must be profound. The mother is also his dearest beloved and his mirror, just as she is for the girl child.

He wanted his mother's imaginary phallus but found he had deceived himself; she possessed, instead, a dark, secret place of which he was so afraid that he had hastily to seal it up before it engulfed him. But the existence of this unstoppable hole makes him perpetually dissatisfied with his own equipment. He wants a bigger, a yet bigger one and rummages around in the chest in which he keeps his dildos, a chest like the one Saint-Ange keeps in her boudoir filled with dildos of every size, he searches to find one that will be big enough to console him for his fear of castration, a phallus of the size with which he adorns his heroes and also his heroines.

But, the more immense the organ with which he equips himself, the greater grows the abyss into which it must plunge. In order to fuck his mother, he needs the most massive dildo in the world; and still it will not satisfy her. Still she will not die of it. Still she will not come; for, when the anatomy lesson, the misanthropy lesson, the lesson in politics, in rage, in terror, is over, we must send her back to her husband, to Father, to whom she belongs.

Home again, home again, fast as you can.

So Mother is exile in perpetuity from this world in the locked, rotting castle of her flesh. We may not fully enjoy her. Exhaustion will always intervene. 'It's finished . . . over . . . oh, why must weakness succeed passions so alive?' There is no solace for the libertine's insatiability because access to the object of love is always denied him. Eugénie's transgression initially disrupts but finally restores the status quo. Mother has not been eroticised. Eugénie has destroyed, spoiled what she could not possess, exorcised the ghost of her first love and now she can exist freely in this world.

Has she not her father's permission to do so?

Home again, home again, fast as you can, my lovely Mama, to the husband who has prepared this instructive afternoon for you.

For Eugénie's transgression is authorised. It is her graduation exercise at the school of love in which her father has enrolled her. Her mother arrives at the academy in order to remove her from it shortly after the delivery of a letter from the licentious de Mistival himself, authorising his wife's martyrisation. When they strip her, they discover her husband has just roundly whipped her. They may do with her whatever they please; Father has told them so. The boudoir, the temple of vice, is a Garden of Eden in which God has permitted the consumption of the fruit of the tree of the knowledge of good and evil.

So, finally, the violation of the mother is no more than a performance, a show; it demonstrates and creates Eugénie's autonomy but also the limits of her autonomy, for her freedom is well policed by the faceless authority beyond the nursery, outside the mirror, the father who knows all, sees all and permits almost everything, except absolute freedom.

The boudoir is a privileged place where these dangerous experiments in synthesising freedom may be conducted in safety. Eugénie does not place herself at real risk by her experiments, nor does she put her companions at risk by aspiring, with her new-found independence, to acts which would put them in jeopardy. She attacks only that part of herself, her reproductive function, she can afford to lose. The taboo against the mother is truly broken once and once only and that is when Eugénie penetrates her mother with the dildo.

Were Madame de Mistival to have come, then all the dykes would be breached at once and chaos and universal night instantly descend; pleasure would have asserted itself triumphantly over pain and the necessity for the existence of repression as a sexual stimulant would have ceased to exist. There would arise the possibility of a world in which the concept of taboo is meaningless and pornography itself would cease to exist. Sade, the prisoner who created freedom in the model of his prison, would have put himself out of business; he is as much afraid of freedom as the next man. So he makes her faint.

He makes her faint because he can only conceive of freedom as existing in opposition, freedom as defined by tyranny. So, on the very edge of an extraordinary discovery about the nature of the relation between mothers and daughters, at the climax of his pioneering exploration of this most obscure of psychic areas, he gives in to a principle of safety. Instead of constructing a machine for liberation, he substitutes instead a masturbatory device. He is on the point of becoming a revolutionary pornography; but he, finally, lacks the courage.

He reverts, now, to being a simple pornographer.

Moreover, the old lag is always imprisoned, even when he is out of his cell, by his own perversion. His perversion, that is an unnatural obsession with pain, is almost like a magic circle which he has constructed around himself to preserve himself from the terrible freedom to which his ideas might lay him open. If 'art is the perpetual immoral subversion of the established order', then why, having gone so far, why not now let Madame de Mistival be overcome by the passions which surround her? Could not the object of genital hatred become the object of genital love? Why does this notion upset him so?

But the taboo against the mother has been violated only to be immediately and hideously restored. The obscenities and profanations never quite fulfil the subversion implicit in them. Shall we prescribe or proscribe this book to our daughters? Sade dithers.

Father must know all, authorise all, or else Eugénie might truly take possession of her autonomy and, say, sheer off Dolmancé's prick, transform him for ever to the condition to which he aspires when he spreads out beneath the handsome virility of the Chevalier, and so truly exercise for herself the phallic mastery at which Sade, Dolmancé himself and her own father assure her she has just arrived.

She savages her mother in order to achieve sexual autonomy, according to the rules of the academy; to attack Father or his substitutes in order to achieve existential autonomy is against the rules. Eugénie's sexual egoism must be sanctioned by the group in which she participates; it must be observed. It must be contained by their observation or else it might threaten the rules of the school itself.

The Sadeian woman, then, subverts only her own socially conditioned role in the world of god, the king and the law. She does not subvert her society, except incidentally, as a storm trooper of the individual consciousness. She remains in the area of privilege created by her class, just as Sade remains in the philosophic framework of his time.

Nevertheless, Sade suggests a type of Oedipal conflict in relation to the mother which is not restricted by gender. Eugénie enacts the crime of Oedipus in a richly psychotic trance; she both copulates with her mother and effectively murders her. In this bewildering dream, Mother becomes the essential primal object, subsuming both parents to herself, as Durand, the phallic and non-reproductive mother, also did.

And, perhaps, in spite of the instructions he sends by his messenger, Father is always absent from this scenario because, in fact, he does not exist.

II KLEINIAN APPENDIX: LIBERTY, MISANTHROPY AND THE BREAST

> The struggle between life and death instincts and the ensuing threat of annihilation of the self and of the object by destructive impulses are fundamental factors in the infant's initial relation to his mother. For his desires imply that the breast and soon the mother should do away with these destructive impulses and the pain of persecutory anxiety.
>
> *Envy and Gratitude*, Melanie Klein

Eugénie's transgression is an exemplary vengeance upon the very idea of the good, a vengeance upon the primal 'good' object, the body of the mother. In the terms of the analysis of Melanie Klein, 'good breast' is the prototype of the fountain of all nourishment; the breast that Sade's libertines take such delight in whipping, upon which they take such derisive glee in wiping their arses, is, as Freud says, 'the place where love and hunger meet', a moving symbol of the existence and the satisfaction of the most basic of all human needs. The body of the mother is the great, good place, the concretisation of the earthly paradise; these fantasies, according to Klein, enrich the primal object, the first thing we meet when we come out of the womb, the great, good place in which we lived without knowing it. The experience of the primal object becomes the foundation for trust, hope and a belief in the existence of good.

Sade/Eugénie profanes the primal object in the conviction that hope, trust and the good are delusions.

'Envy contributes to the infant's difficulties in building up a good object, for he feels that the gratification of which he was deprived has been kept for himself by the breast that frustrated him,' says Melanie Klein. This envy may manifest itself in violent attacks on the mother's body. Envy, jealousy and greed are the vices of early childhood. If envy implies the subject's relation with one other person only and a desire to rob that person of a desirable possession, or, if robbing is impossible, at least to spoil it, so that nobody else may benefit from it, then jealousy implies a more peopled landscape and a relation to at least two people. Envy and greed are our first negative emotions; we envy the breast its abundance and greedily wish to drink it dry. Jealousy implies a degree of maturing; we now perceive something other than the breast and ourselves, we perceive a third. The experience of jealousy marks the point at which the solipsistic accord between child and mother ceases. Life as a social being begins.

We are jealous because we feel there is only a limited amount of love available and somebody else may secure it all. Eugénie sews up her mother so that she will not be able to produce any little brothers and sisters; Madame de Mistival must undergo this ordeal in order to remove the desolating notion of the arrival of rivals who will jostle Eugénie for attention for themselves and deprive her of unique nourishment. But Madame de Mistival is already possessed by Eugénie's own father; she bears the marks of his possession on her body, he has beaten her until her buttocks look like watered silk, to show how absolute is his right to the use of her flesh and the degree to which her flesh affects him by its insubornable separateness from him. Eugénie's rage is no different at source from her father's rage. The libertine frenzy of father and daughter in Sade's parable spring from greed, envy and jealousy, a helpless rage at the organs of generation that bore us into a world of pain where the enjoyment of the senses is all that can alleviate the daily horror of living. In the introduction to *Philosophy in the Boudoir*, Sade writes: 'It is only by sacrificing everything to sensual pleasure that this being known as Man, cast into the world in spite of himself, may succeed in sowing a few roses on the thorns of life.'

Sade's quarrel, therefore, is not only with the mother, who can deprive him of love and sustenance at will; it is the very fact of generation that he finds intolerable. In the short story, '*Eugénie de Franval*', Franval denies his daughter's right to marry and have children: 'Then you think the human race should be allowed to die out?' his wife asks him. 'Why not?' he replies. 'A planet whose only product is poison cannot be rooted out too quickly.'

The Sadeian libertine cannot forgive the mother, not for what she is, but for what she has done – for having thoughtlessly, needlessly inflicted life upon him. Therefore he conducts his irreconcilable existence entirely upon a metaphysical plane; his whole life is a violent protest against an irreversible condition because, though it is easy to stop living, it is impossible to erase the fact of one's birth. One may not remove oneself from history, though Sade tried to do it. His will directs he should be buried in a ditch, and 'the ditch, once covered over, about it acorns shall be strewn, in order that the spot become green again, and the copse grown back thick over it, the traces of my grave may disappear from the face of the earth, as I trust the memory of me shall fade out of the minds of all men.'

Rage and despair of this quality has a heroic monumentality; but, in his work, Sade is finally ambivalent. Eugénie seals up her mother to keep the dangerous infection of fecundity from spilling into the world but she does not, dare not, excise the womb where the child is produced. Let us quarantine the fecund woman; let us keep her out of sexual circulation, so she does not allow a fallen race to continue to perpetuate its miseries. But we will not go quite so far as to sterilise her completely – because Sade is still in complicity with the authority which he hates.

FIVE

Speculative Finale:
The Function of Flesh

> . . . the process of human cultural development, in which sexuality remains the weak spot.
>
> *Three Essays on the Theory of Sexuality*,
> Sigmund Freud

The word 'fleisch', in German, provokes me to an involuntary shudder. In the English language, we make a fine distinction between flesh, which is usually alive and, typically, human; and meat, which is dead, inert, animal and intended for consumption. Substitute the word 'flesh' in the Anglican service of Holy Communion; 'Take, eat, this is my meat which was given for you . . .' and the sacred comestible becomes the offering of something less than, rather than more than, human. 'Flesh' in English carries with it a whole system of human connotations and the flesh of the Son of Man cannot be animalised into meat without an inharmonious confusion of meaning. But, because it is human, flesh is also ambiguous; we are adjured to shun the world, the flesh and the Devil. Fleshly delights are lewd distractions from the contemplation of higher, that is, of spiritual, things; the pleasures of the flesh are vulgar and unrefined, even with an element of beastliness about them, although flesh tints have the sumptuous succulence of peaches because flesh plus skin equals sensuality.

But, if flesh plus skin equals sensuality, then flesh minus skin equals meat. The skin has turned into rind, or crackling; the garden of fleshly delights becomes a butcher's shop, or Sweeney Todd's kitchen. My flesh encounters your taste for meat. So much the worse for me.

What are the butcherly delights of meat? These are not sensual but analytical. The satisfaction of scientific curiosity in dissection. A clinical pleasure in the precision with which the process of reducing the living, moving, vivid object to the dead status of thing is accomplished. The pleasure of watching the spectacle of the slaughter that derives from the knowledge one is dissociated from the spectacle; the bloody excitation of the audience in the abattoir, who watch the dramatic transformation act, from living flesh to dead meat, derives from the knowledge they are safe from the knife themselves. There is the technical pleasure of carving and the anticipatory pleasure of the prospect of eating the meat, of the assimilation of the dead stuff, after which it will be humanly transformed into flesh.

Flesh has specific orifices to contain the prick that penetrates it but meat's relation to the knife is more random and a thrust anywhere will do. Sade explores the inhuman sexual possibilities of meat; it is a mistake to think that the substance of which his actors are made is flesh. There is nothing alive or sensual about them. Sade is a great puritan and will disinfect of

162

sensuality anything he can lay his hands on; therefore he writes about sexual relations in terms of butchery and meat.

The murderous attacks on the victims demonstrate the abyss between the parties to the crime, an abyss of incomprehension that cannot be bridged. The lamb does not understand why it is led to the slaughter and so it goes willingly, because it is in ignorance. Even when it dawns on the lamb that it is going to be killed, the lamb only struggles because it does not understand that it cannot escape; and, besides, it is hampered by the natural ignorance of the herbivore, who does not even know it is possible to eat meat. The lamb could understand easily enough how mint sauce might be delicious but it does not have the mental apparatus to appreciate that its own hindquarters are also nourishing food if suitably cooked, for those with different tastes. Which is why we prefer to eat the herbivores. Because, under no circumstances, could they eat us.

The relations between men and women are often distorted by the reluctance of both parties to acknowledge that the function of flesh is meat to the carnivore but not grass to the herbivore.

The ignorance of one party as to the intentions of the other makes the victim so defenceless against predation that it can seem as if a treacherous complicity finally unites them; as though, in some sense, the victim wills a victim's fate. But, if any of the Sadeian victims seem to incite their masters to their violence by tacitly accepting their right to administer it, let us not make too much of this apparent complicity. There is no defence at all against absolute tyranny.

Constance, most abused of all the wives in *The Hundred and Twenty Days at Sodom*, seeing she has no choice, cleans out her husband's arsehole with her tongue. 'And the poor creature, only too accustomed to these horrors, carried them out as a dutiful, a thoughtful wife, should; ah, great God! what will not dread and thralldom produce.' Absolute tyranny is, by definition, absolute; once the victims, seized by force, enter the impregnable castle, they are already as good as dead. Minski, the cannibal giant, tells Juliette that she and her companions are in his power, to do with as he pleases, as soon as they enter his island fortress. Don Clement warns Justine that any resistance to the masters in the church of St Mary-in-the-Wood is useless. The Chateau of Silling, the imitation Sodom, is utterly impregnable and the paths that brought the victims there have been destroyed behind them. The victims have been erased from the world and now live, their own ghosts although they are not yet dead, only awaiting death, in a world where the function of their own flesh is to reveal to them the gratuitous inevitability of pain, to demonstrate the shocking tragedy of mortality itself, that all flesh may be transformed, at any moment, to meat.

Necrophagy is the exposition of the meatiness of human flesh. Necrophagy parodies the sacramental meal by making its assumptions real. The fifteen-year-old boy roasted for dinner at Minski's house is served up without ceremony; for Minski, he is nothing more nor less than a good meal. Minski claims he owes his health, strength, youthful appearance and abundant seminal secretions to his habitual diet of other people. Cannibalism, the most elementary act of exploitation, that of turning the other directly into a comestible; of seeing the other in the most primitive terms of use.

The strong abuse, exploit and meatify the weak, says Sade. They must and will devour their natural prey. The primal condition of man cannot be modified in any way; it is, eat or be eaten. Eat, assimilate; but the process doesn't stop there. Defecate, assimilate again. How greedily the coprophile consumes the physical surplus of the act of eating.

Only the most violent of all transformations, that of the transformation of the Kingdom of God into a secular republic will overthrow these relations. In the Kingdom of God, man is made in the image of God and therefore a ravenous, cannibalistic, vicious, egocentric tyrant. Since God does not exist, man must make of himself something a great deal better; that God must be *shown* not to exist, and only corrupts our institutions as a baleful shadow, is the source of Sade's passionate and continual atheism. The Kingdom of God and the secular Republic are notions that transcend monarchy, religion and democracy; they are to do with authoritarianism and libertarianism.

In this world, which was made by God, sexuality is inhuman. In other words, in a society which still ascribes an illusory metaphysic to matters which are in reality solely to do with the relations between human beings, the expression of the sexual nature of men and women is not seen as part of human nature. Sexuality, in this estranged form, becomes a denial of a basis of mutuality, of the acknowledgement of equal rights to exist in the world, from which any durable form of human intercourse can spring.

Sexuality, stripped of the idea of free exchange, is not in any way humane; it is nothing but pure cruelty. Carnal knowledge is the infernal knowledge of the flesh as meat. The fruit of the tree of the knowledge of good and evil is cooked up and served for breakfast in Minski's house in the form of testicle patties and virgin's blood sausages.

So flesh becomes meat by a magical transition about which there is nothing natural. Nobody in Sade's pornography dies of natural causes, of old age or sickness. Death is always a violent infliction by another, or even by Nature itself. Or perhaps, rather, death is always 'natural' since Nature itself is a murderer. When the thunderbolt strikes down Justine, Nature has murdered the girl as effectively as the libertines could have done. In Sade, Nature is a version of the Cruel God of the Old Testament.

Death, in Sade, is always the sudden, violent metamorphosis of the vivid into the inert. Death is always such an outrage, such a crime, such an impiety that Sade must have found it as hard to reconcile himself to the fact of mortality as he did to the fact of birth.

The act of predation – the butcher's job of rendering the flesh of the victim into meat for the table, which Minski himself performs in an exemplary fashion by the violence of his very act of copulation – is the assertion of the abyss between master and victim. There is no question of reciprocal sensation; the idea of it is abhorrent to the Sadeian libertine, except under certain special circumstances where *two of a kind* meet and perform rituals of which both understand the significance. In these cases, violence is a form of play. Otherwise, the dichotomy between active and passive, evil and good, is absolute, and, what is more, perceived as unchanging, an immutable division between classes.

Reciprocity of sensation is not possible because to share is to be robbed.

Dom Clement the monk outlines an economic theory of the nature of sexual pleasure to Justine during her stay in his establishment. Just as Juliette was so rich that she could not afford to give alms, so Clement argues that there is not enough pleasure to go round and he must have it all. If I give anybody else any of my pleasure, I will diminish my own, just as, if I give you half my apple, then I shall only have half left for myself. Pleasure may never be shared, or it will be diminished. A shared pleasure is a betrayal of the self, a seeping away of some of the subject's precious egotism. To share is to be stolen from, says Clement; when a woman pilfers her sexual pleasure from a man, she patently reduces his own and to witness her pleasure can do nothing more for him than to flatter his vanity.

Since gratified vanity is a pleasure of sentimental affect only and therefore inferior to the real pleasure of the senses, it is to be despised. Besides, a man's vanity may be flattered in a far more piquant manner by harshly denying a woman any pleasure at all and forcing her to minister only to the man's pleasure, at the cost of her visible pain. 'In one word, is not he who imposes much more surely the master than he who shares?' The nature of Clement's pleasure is by no means a sensual one; his pleasure is a cerebral one, even an intellectual one – that of the enhancement of the ego. When pleasure is violently denied the partner, the self's pleasure is enhanced in direct relation to the visible unpleasure of the victim. And so the self knows it exists.

Sexual pleasure, therefore, consists primarily in the submission of the partner; but that is not enough. The annihilation of the partner is the only sufficient proof of the triumph of the ego. Dolmancé declares that an erection is sufficient in itself to make a man a despot; pride, says Dolmancé, causes a man 'to wish to be the only one in the world capable of experiencing what he feels; the idea of seeing another enjoy as he enjoys reduces him to a kind of equality with that other which impairs the unspeakable charm *despotism* inspires in him.'

The uniquely unselfing experience of orgasm may be enjoyed to the full only when it is experienced uniquely; perhaps only when there is nobody to observe the loss of self in the orgasm. Dolmancé prefers to take women from behind, in a position where he cannot see or be seen.

Now the sexual act becomes a matter of extreme privacy, in which only the nervous agitation of the partner who experiences the strongest sensation during intercourse has any significance. The despot inflicts sex on the slave and he is perfectly justified in doing so. Dolmancé opines that nature intends man to feel superior, to be a despot, and that is why man is physically stronger than woman. Further, the orgasm is experienced as a fury because nature intends that 'behaviour during copulation should be the same as behaviour in anger'.

Wreaking an impotent fury on an object that may not respond because it has been stunned into submission, he gnaws, bites and soils the loved and hated flesh. All men want to molest women during sexual activity, says Dolmancé; that is the sign of their natural superiority to them.

Remember that this lecture is given to an audience of women; Saint-Ange and Eugénie listen and applaud; since he is good enough to class them with the masters, they, too, will be permitted to tyrannise as much as they please. Libido, since it is sex itself, is genderless; vessels of undiluted libido, these super-women are included amongst the aggressors, the unique individuals who follow the desolating logic of the imagination to that lonely pitch of phallic supremacy up above the world in as awesome and rigorous a puritanism as Simeon Stylites on his pole. This is a conspiracy of carnivores. 'We, you, Madame, and I, those like ourselves – we are the only people who deserve to be listened to!'

Dolmancé, however, has so greatly excited himself with his own discourse that he is forced to break off and bugger Augustin, the gardener. All present execute another geometric exercise and ejaculate in unison. But the presence of his fellow-conspirators in the group games does not alleviate the solitude of the libertine; rather, it enhances it. The libertine's sovereign orgasm is not shared with his fellow libertines; it simply occurs at the same time. The parallel if simultaneous orgasms of the libertines cannot intersect with one another. There is no fusion to confuse, to interfere with the unique experience.

In Sade, sexual pleasure is an entirely inward experience. Roles may be changed about and women become men, men women; the whipper will be whipped in his turn. But the territoriality of the subject's pleasure cannot be invaded because sexual pleasure is nothing but a private and individual shock of the nerves. Noirceuil defines pleasure: 'What is pleasure? Simply this: that which occurs when voluptuous atoms, or atoms emanated from voluptuous objects, clash with and fire the electrical particles circulating in the hollow of our nerve fibres. To complete the pleasure the clash must be as violent as possible.' This is a form of exacerbated auto-eroticism. Sexual pleasure is not experienced *as* experience; it does not modify the subject. An entirely externally induced phenomenon, its sensation is absolutely personal, just as it does not hurt the knife if you cut yourself with it.

Yet, curiously enough, Sade himself is the lamb led to slaughter as well as the butcher with the insensible knife. In the

well-documented events of a certain morning in 1772 in a bedroom in Marseilles, the hired girl flogged Sade with a heather
broom; he marked the number of blows with his knife in the
mantelpiece. Then, while he coupled with the girl, his valet
buggered him. Throughout the Cytherean morning, the girl
stated, he addressed his servant as 'Monsieur le Marquis', elementary transformation of pain and pleasure, aristocrat and
servant. Dolmancé gasps to Saint-Ange's brother: 'Deign, Oh
my love, to serve me as a woman after having been my lover.'
He presents Eugénie de Mistival with her weapon; an india-
rubber dildo, with which to bugger him. When he whips her, he
consoles Eugénie with the assertion of a dialectic of mutual
aggression: 'Now victim for a moment, my lovely angel, soon
you'll persecute me in your turn.'

These violent transformations of appearance are the only
ways in which Sade can envisage reciprocity. Mutual aggression
can never take place at the same time but only in a serial fashion, now me, now you, and the cock, the phallus, the sceptre of
a virility which is not a state-in-itself, in fact, however phallo-
centric the notion of sexuality implicit in Sade's pornography
might be, but a modality, is passed from man to woman, woman
to man, man to man, woman to woman, back and forth, as in a
parlour game.

We must not confuse these parlour games with those kinds of
real relations that change you. Sexual activity in these Sadeian
communities of equals is a social exploit, a communal activity,
an infertility festival, with a choric quality. It has certain relations to kinetic art. The libertines assemble themselves in
architectonic configurations, fuck furiously, discharge all
together – all fall down. They have arranged themselves as for

a group photograph, and it is the most complicated mechanics that must set the erotic engine in motion, mouth against cunt, cock in anus, tongue on testicles, finger on clitoris (whose sexual function is not a discovery of the twentieth century). Like a good housewife organising her store cupboard, Sade wants a place for everything and everything in its place in the regimented pursuit of pleasure.

Suitably garbed for these pornographic occasions in kitsch uniforms of gauze, assembled in voluptuous boudoirs or arranged like sacrilegious offerings upon the altars of churches, the libertines perform extraordinary tableaux with well-drilled precision. Among this well-populated activity, there is as little room for intimacy as there is upon the football field.

The bed is now as public as the dinner table and governed by the same rules of formal confrontation. Flesh has lost its common factor; that it is the substance of which we are all made and yet that differentiates us. It has acquired, instead, the function of confusing kind and gender, man and beast, woman and fowl. The subject itself becomes an *objet de luxe* in these elaborately choreographed masques of abstraction, of alienation.

The libertine goes to the orgy to enhance his notion of his unique and supreme self; but, only in the group, among his peers, is the self truly lost. Where desire is a function of the act rather than the act a function of desire, desire loses its troubling otherness; it ceases to be a movement outwards from the self. The arrows of desire are turned back on the heart, and pierce it.

For the libertine chooses to surround himself, not with lovers or partners, but with accomplices. The libertine would not trust a partner, who would rob him of pleasure by causing him to feel rather than to experience.

The presence of his accomplices preserves his ego from the singular confrontation with the object of a reciprocal desire which is, in itself, both passive object and active subject. Such a partner acts on us as we act on it; both partners are changed by the exchange and, if submission is mutual, then aggression is mutual. Such a partner might prove to the libertine that sexuality is an aspect of being, rather than a crime against being; but the libertine doesn't, after all, want to know that. If the evidence of Sade's ingrained puritanism is that he believes sex in itself to be a crime, and associates its expression with violent crime, the libertine's entire pleasure is the cerebral, not sensual one, of knowing he is engaging in forbidden activity. It is the presence of his accomplices, all engaged on the same project, that convinces him he commits a crime. The knowledge that sexuality is criminal preserves him from the onslaught of love.

If he were not criminal, he would be forced to abdicate from his position as the lord of creation, made in the image of God; his criminality is his excuse, the source of his pride, and of his denial of love.

The libertine's perversions are the actings-out of his denial of love. Yet Freud suggests the 'mental factor' plays a large part in accomplishing the transformation of the instinctual desire for simple sensual pleasure in the case of necrophily, coprophily and bestiality. The Sadeian libertine is proudly conscious of such activities as 'perversions', even as he strenuously denies the actual concept of perversion; that to eat shit and screw corpses and dogs are not the pastimes of the common man is part of his pride in doing so himself. Yet this transformation of the appetite in favour of the initially unappetising is human work, not criminal work. Freud says: 'It is impossible to deny that . . . a piece of work has been performed which, in spite of its horrifying result, is the equivalent of an idealisation of the instinct. The omnipotence of love is perhaps never more strongly proved than in such of its aberrations as these.'

The excremental enthusiasm of the libertines transforms the ordure in which they roll to a bed of roses. The pleasure of the libertine philosophers derives in a great part from the knowledge they have overcome their initial disgust. By the exercise of the will, they have overcome repugnance and so, in one sense, are liberated from the intransigence of reality. This liberation from reality is their notion of freedom; the way to freedom lies through the privy. But the conquest of morality and aesthetics, of shame, disgust and fear, the pursuit of greater and greater sexual sophistication in terms of private sensation lead them directly to the satisfactions of the child; transgression becomes regression and, like a baby, they play with their own excrement.

Even the pursuit of the vilest of all passions, the murderous passions, lead them back to the cradle in the end; they have not acquired these tastes in the process of maturing. They had only forgotten them. Now, freed from all adult restraint, they remember them again. 'It may be assumed that the impulse of cruelty arises from the instinct for mastery and appears at a period of sexual life at which the genitals have not yet taken over their later role,' suggests Freud. The shamelessness and violence of the libertines is that of little children who are easily cruel because they have not learned the capacity for pity which the libertines dismiss as 'childish' because the libertines themselves have not yet grown up enough to acknowledge the presence of others in their solipsistic world.

Juliette, as Theodor Adorno and Max Horkheimer say,

embodies 'intellectual pleasure in regression'. She attacks civil-isation with its own weapons. She exercises rigorously rational thought; she creates systems; she exhibits an iron self-control. Her will triumphs over the barriers of pain, shame, disgust and morality until her behaviour reverts to the polymorphous per-versity of the child, who has not yet learnt the human objections to cruelty because, in a social sense, no child is yet fully human. Her destination has always been her commence-ment. The triumph of the will recreates, as its Utopia, the world of early childhood, and that is a world of nightmare, impotence and fear, in which the child fantasises, out of its own power-lessness, an absolute supremacy.

Yet the adult world of work may not be evaded; but it, too, is transformed. Sexual satisfaction may be obtained only at the cost of enormous expenditures of energy. Pleasure is a hard task-master. *The Hundred and Twenty Days at Sodom* offers a black version of the Protestant ethic but the profit, the orgasm obtained with so much effort, the product of so much pain and endeavour – the pursuit of this profit leads directly to hell. To a perfectly material hell. The final murderous passion recounted by Desgranges is called the 'hell-game'. The liber-tine, assisted by torturers disguised as demons, himself pretends to be the devil; Juliette similarly dresses Saint Fond as a demon during an orgy. If we once needed the notion of a hell in order to console ourselves that something exists worse than this world, we no longer need it now.

The elaboration of pleasure will change its quality; the simple passions of the libertines in Duclos's accounts in the first book will elaborate insensibly, will become the complex atroc-ities of the third book.

To obtain his precious orgasm, the libertine must now hunt it down single-mindedly through seas of blood and excrement. But, the more earnestly he strives, the further the goal recedes from him. He is forced to invest more and more energy in the pursuit of orgasm; all the same, it grows harder and harder for him to come. His rituals become more elaborate, his needs more abstract. The structure of his own invented reality hardens around him and imprisons him. The passions he thought would free him from the cage of being become the very bars of the cage that traps him; he himself cannot escape the theatrical decor he has created around himself in order to give himself the confidence to immolate his victims. During the hell-game, the libertine is himself as much in hell as his victims are and they can at least escape from it by dying. He cannot.

Sade's eroticism, with its tragic style, its displays, its cortèges, its sacrifices, its masks and costumes, preserves something of the demonology of primitive man. The libertines are indeed like men possessed by demons. Their orgasms are like the visitation of the gods of Voodoo, annihilating, appalling. Minski's orgasm, that kills his partners, is announced by a ringing yell. Catherine the Great screams and blasphemes. Durand emits dreadful screams and her limbs twitch and thresh; she seems to have succumbed to a fit. Saint Fond's shrieks, his contortions, his blasphemies are appalling and he half faints at the climax. These descriptions are those of torture; this is 'the precious climax, which characterises the enjoyment as good or bad.'

The return to the self after such a crisis must be a lowering passage. Orgasm has possessed the libertine; during the irreducible timelessness of the moment of orgasm, the hole in the world through which we fall, he has been as a god, but this state is as fearful as it is pleasurable and, besides, is lost as soon as it is attained. He has burst into the Utopia of desire, in which only the self exists; he has not negotiated the terms of his arrival there, as gentle lovers do, but taken Utopia by force. See, the conquering hero comes. And, just as immediately, he has been expelled from it, a fall like Lucifer's, from heaven to hell.

The annihilation of the self and the resurrection of the body, to die in pain and to painfully return from death, is the sacred drama of the Sadeian orgasm. In this drama, flesh is used instrumentally, to provoke these spasmodic visitations of dreadful pleasure. In this flesh, nothing human remains; it aspires to the condition of the sacramental meal. It is never the instrument of love.

In his diabolic solitude, only the possibility of love could awake the libertine to perfect, immaculate terror. It is in this holy terror of love that we find, in both men and women themselves, the source of all opposition to the emancipation of women.

Postscript:
Red Emma Replies to
the Madman of Charenton

History tells us that every oppressed class gained true lib-eration from its masters through its own efforts. It is necessary that woman learn that lesson, that she realise that her freedom will reach as far as her power to achieve her freedom reaches. It is, therefore, far more important for her to begin with her inner regeneration, to cut loose from the weight of prejudices, traditions, and customs. The demand for equal rights in every voca-tion of life is just and fair; but, after all, the most vital right is the right to love and be loved. Indeed, if partial emancipation is to become a complete and true emanci-pation of woman, it will have to do away with the ridiculous notion that to be loved, to be sweetheart and mother, is synonymous with being slave or subordinate. It will have to do away with the absurd notion of the dualism of the sexes, or that man and woman represent two antagonistic worlds.

Pettiness separates, breadth unites. Let us be broad and big. Let us not overlook vital things because of the bulk of trifles confronting us. A true conception of the relation of the sexes will not admit of conqueror and conquered; it knows of but one great thing: to give of one's self boundlessly, in order to find one's self richer, deeper, better. That alone can fill the emptiness, and transform the tragedy of woman's emancipation into joy, limitless joy.

The Tragedy of Woman's Emancipation,
Emma Goldman

BIBLIOGRAPHY

SADE'S WORK

Oeuvres complètes, 16 vols. (Cercle du Livre Précieux, Paris, 1966–7)

TRANSLATIONS

The Complete Justine, Philosophy in the Bedroom and other writings, tr. Richard Seaver and Austryn Wainhouse (Grove Press, New York, 1965)
The Hundred and Twenty Days at Sodom (Grove Press, New York, 1966)
Juliette (Grove Press, New York, 1968)

OTHER SOURCES

The Dialectics of Enlightenment, Theodor Adorno and Max Horkheimer, tr. John Cumming (Allen Lane, London, 1973)
Sade/Fourier/Loyola, Roland Barthes, tr. Richard Miller (Jonathan Cape, London, 1977)
L'Erotisme, Georges Bataille (Editions de Minuit, Paris, 1957)

Must we Burn Sade?, Simone de Beauvoir, with selections from his writings chosen by Paul Dinnage (John Calder, London, 1962)

Anthologie de l'Humeur Noir, ed. André Breton, Jean Jacques Pauvert (Paris, 1966)

Symbolic Wounds, Bruno Bettelheim (Thames and Hudson, London, 1955)

Life against Death: the Psychoanalytical Meaning of History, Norman O. Brown (Routledge & Kegan Paul, London, 1959)

Black Skin White Masks, Frantz Fanon (MacGibbon & Kee, London, 1968)

Love and Death in the American Novel, Leslie Fiedler (Jonathan Cape, London, 1967)

Madness and Civilisation: a History of Insanity in the Age of Reason, Michel Foucault, tr. Richard Howard (Tavistock Publications, London, 1965)

Introductory Lectures on Psychoanalysis, Sigmund Freud, tr. James Strachey (Hogarth Press, London, revised edition of 1962)

New Introductory Lectures on Psychoanalysis, Sigmund Freud, tr. James Strachey (Hogarth Press, London, revised edition of 1962)

Beyond the Pleasure Principle, Sigmund Freud, tr. James Strachey (Hogarth Press, London, edition of 1961)

Three Essays on the Theory of Sexuality, Sigmund Freud, tr. James Strachey (Hogarth Press, London, revised edition of 1962)

The Life and Ideas of the Marquis de Sade, Geoffrey Gorer (Panther, London, 1964)

Norma Jean: the story of Marilyn Monroe, Fred Lawrence Guiles (W. H. Allen, London, 1969)

Leviathan, Thomas Hobbes, edited by C. B. Macpherson (Penguin, London, 1968)

Envy and Gratitude, Melanie Klein (Tavistock Publications, London, 1957)

'Kant avec Sade', Jacques Lacan, essay in *Ecrits II* (Editions de Seuil, Paris, 1971)

Marquis de Sade, Gilbert Lely, tr. Alec Brown (Paul Elek, London, 1961)

Psychoanalysis and Feminism, Juliet Mitchell (Allen Lane, London, 1974)

Marilyn, Norman Mailer (Hodder and Stoughton, London, 1973)

Not in God's Image, Julia O'Faolain and Lauro Martines (Temple Smith, London, 1973)

Art and Pornography, Morse Peckham (Basic Books, New York, 1969)

The Complete Works of François Rabelais, tr. Sir Thomas Urquhart and Peter Motteux (Bodley Head, London, 1933)

The Marquis de Sade, Donald Thomas (Weidenfeld and Nicholson, London, 1977)

Earth Spirit, and Pandora's Box, Frank Wedekind, tr. Stephen Spender (Calder and Boyars, London, 1972)

Anarchism and Other Essays, Emma Goldman, with a new introduction by Richard Drinnon (Dover Publications, New York, 1969)